CENTRAL STATION

CENTRAL STATION

Realizing a Vision

How an Abandoned Railroad Yard Became Chicago's Largest Mixed-Use Community

GERALD W. FOGELSON
Co-Chairman and CEO of Central Station Development Corp.

with JOE MARCONI

Racom Communications
Evanston, Illinois

Library of Congress Cataloging-in-Publication Data
available from the Library of Congress.
Project Management: Richard Hagle
Design and Typesetting: Sans Serif, Inc.

Published by Racom Communications
815 Ridge Ave., Evanston, IL 60202
Copyright © 2003 by Gerald W. Fogelson

International Standard Book Number: 0-9704515-0-2

To my wife Georgia, who has been there every step of the way
And to the memory of Leonard Schanfield,
A great mentor and a man who helped me turn a dream into reality

Contents

Foreword

What sets aside a "producer" from ordinary people? A developer performs the same functions as a theatrical or cinema producer, and much, much more.

Many of us were exposed to the opportunities of the area now known as Central Station, but Jerry Fogelson, with the enthusiastic backing of one of the smartest men extant in American real estate, Albert Ratner, CEO of Forest City Enterprises of Cleveland, Ohio, has achieved an overwhelmingly successful real estate development and the transformation of Chicago's south side into one of the greatest living areas in America.

Richard Daley, a Mayor in love with his city, and Burt Natarus, Alderman and political leader, have wholeheartedly supported Jerry's dream.

Jerry's team of highly professional architects, planners, contractors, and other experts has been molded by the driving perseverance of this highly focused and determined man whose foresight saw a great potential and had the personal talent to bring the development of Central Station to fruition.

A standing ovation for a tremendously well-conceived, well-planned and well-executed contribution to this great City of Chicago.

—*Marshall Bennett*

Introduction

This book tells the story of Central Station, 80-plus acres of Chicago's past, present and future. Beginning with a brief history of the Illinois Central Railroad's role in the emergence of Chicago as a world class city, this book goes on to describe how we created a plan that imagined the future.

We have, after all, a unique story to tell—starting with a great city property located on a spectacular lakefront, adjoining the fabulous Grant Park and Michigan Avenue, adjacent to McCormick Place—the world's largest convention center—plus a concentration of museums at our property line.

Anyone who has ever built a home has stories they could tell—things that go wrong, arrangements that fall through, stops and starts, changes of all types made along the way. Imagine that multiplied by an entire community. There have been reasons to celebrate, interrupted by times of stress, challenge and personal loss.

Central Station, until the 1980s, was a vast parcel of vacant land and air rights along the railroad tracks that had once been a receiving yard and a train depot. It was the only lakefront land that *was not* included in the famous Daniel Burnham Plan for the City of Chicago.

In 1989, the Central Station Limited Partnership acquired the land and air rights that we would later develop into a multibillion-dollar, mixed-use real estate complex and Chicago's largest community. Many people played important roles, from those who did their jobs to those who are making this property their homes. For all who have worked so hard and all who will live, work and enjoy this unusual and historic property . . . *Welcome to Central Station.*

—*Jerry Fogelson*

A Brief History of the Illinois Central in Chicago

IT STARTED WITH A VACANT RAILROAD YARD ON AN 80-plus acre parcel of land.

Several billion dollars and more than a dozen years later, the land continues to evolve into a vibrant residential, commercial and retail area where people live, work and enjoy unparalleled access to the city's lakefront, parks and cultural center. To better appreciate today's Central Station community, we have to go back to another era.

"Public Ground—A Common to Remain Forever Open, Clear and Free of any Buildings or Other Obstructions whatever."

These words were offered in 1836 by William B. Archer, Gurdon Saltonstall Hubbard and William F. Thornton, three men commissioned by the State of Illinois to sell unsettled land within its borders in order to generate funds to pay for a new shipping canal. They refused to bow to pressure from industrialists to sell the city's lakefront. They made a promise to the people of Chicago, which would be incorporated as a city one year later, to protect its beautiful and treasured shoreline. For nearly 20 years the matter was argued in the courts and in the Illinois state legislature. Then a deal was made that dramatically altered the future of Chicago.

The 1800s were a great time for the railroads of America. For personal travel and the transporting of goods and equipment of every kind, the rails kept the still young nation moving. And Chicago was its emerging heart.

People often quote from Carl Sandburg's *Chicago*, his famous description of the city as "Hog Butcher For The World" and the "City of the Big Shoulders," but no less significant was his recognition of the city as a "Player with Railroads and the Nation's Freight Handler". Some two dozen railroads came to Chicago, but many historians hold that none had as great a social or physical impact on the city as the Illinois Central. Since 1852, the IC has defined the territory along its lines more than any other railroad.

The Deal That Saved Chicago's Lakefront

In 1852, the fight to preserve Chicago's lakefront appeared to be lost when the city council granted a request from the IC, permitting the railroad a lakefront right-of-way to a terminal and freight complex it had purchased on the old Fort Dearborn estate. In exchange, the IC would construct much needed dikes and breakwaters along the Lake Michigan shore. Storms and currents had badly eroded the lake shore area and the parks that fronted the luxurious homes of wealthy South Side residents along Michigan Avenue. Winter and spring gales produced huge walls of water that literally came crashing against the front doors of some of the city's finest homes. Damage was extensive, but the cost of constructing offshore barricades was high, and the city leaders refused to increase the already high taxes to pay for such measures. The IC deal appeared to be a workable solution.

What at first seemed like the end of the city's lakefront proved to be otherwise. Because of erosion, the land the city signed over to the railroad was at that point at the bottom of the lake, not on Chicago's shoreline. The IC was forced to enter the city on a trestle constructed four hundred feet offshore. The two-mile stretch of stone cribs and breakwaters it agreed to build protected both its own elevated tracks and the city's damaged shoreline. To placate the city's elite Michigan Avenue homeowners, the city attempted to convince the IC to fill in the land between its new sea wall and the shore so a new park and promenade could be created. To say the railroad balked at the notion would be an understatement.

Those favoring creation of a lakefront park fought the railroad's attempts to expand and the matter was ultimately resolved in court around the turn of the century, leading to vast shoreline improvements.

In his book *City of the Century: The Epic of Chicago and the Making of America*, Professor Donald L. Miller wrote, " . . . for decades after the Chicago Compromise of 1852, the city's southern lakefront remained the principality of the Illinois Central Railroad. The trains it sent streaming across its Lake Michigan trestle, turning the lakefront into a sooty industrial corridor, were an hourly reminder of who owned Chicago. The railroad received court permission to use additional submerged land at the river's mouth to create a landfill extension of its terminal, storage, and docking facilities [turning the water] . . . into a still pool filled with industrial debris, floating packing crates, and the bloated corpses of horses and cattle."

In *Limiteds Along the Lakefront: The Illinois Central in Chicago*, Alan R. Lind wrote of the IC's great trains "sweeping in from the southwest to meet the lake front at Hyde Park, then running parallel to Lake Michigan all the way to the Chicago River. In the early years the IC trains reached the Great Central Station at South Water Street over a trestle in the lake which ran from 22nd Street to Randolph Street. After the Chicago Fire of 1871, the space between the shore and the trestle was filled with debris from the fire, forming a parcel of land that further expanded to the east to create Chicago's magnificent lakefront park."

Parade by
Central Station

Building the outer bulkhead of the IC in Lake Michigan,
April to August, 1896

Railroad Maps Its Own Success

Beginning in the mid-1800s and for several decades after, the IC seemed to be tracing the property lines of Chicago's business elite whose homes dotted the railroad's path from Michigan Avenue in central Chicago, out along Prairie Avenue, ultimately stretching as far south as Kenwood and Hyde Park.

These were good years for the IC. Growth in the railroad's passenger business kept it continuously outgrowing its facilities. A number of temporary and permanent depots were built during this period. The IC's principal facility, "Central Station," was constructed at 11th Place in 1893, where it stood until its demolition in 1972.

The Illinois Central provides a distinguished chapter in the history of the United States itself, with some of the country's most illustrious figures contributing to the railroad's story—Senator Stephen A. Douglas; financier Edward H. Harriman and his sons, E. Roland and W. Averell Harriman; the legendary detective Allen Pinkerton, who worked for the IC before moving to Washington as the founder of the Secret Service; and General Robert E. Wood. President Abraham Lincoln was once the IC's attorney. The list of prominent leaders of government, business and finance who were associated with the IC through the years must be included among those who shaped America in its second century.

The IC's Central Station Was Built on Innovation

Central Station was the name given to the new IC depot and office building at 11th Place (then called Park Row) and Michigan Avenue. The soft soil on which the structure was built had once been the bottom of Lake Michigan. This meant that new piling techniques had to be devised in order to support the building's enormous weight. Construction began in 1892 and was completed in 1893, less than nine months later, at a cost of $1.2 million. Lovers of railroad history note that it was during that same year that the real Casey Jones, an IC engineer from the South, came to Chicago to run the trains at the 1893 World's Fair.

The architect of Central Station, Bradford L. Gilbert, designed a Romanesque structure with a waiting room characterized by a 45-foot vaulted ceiling, and a 140-foot by 610-foot train shed that was, at the time, the largest such facility in the world. The waiting room's east side featured stained glass pictures of charioteers driving five galloping horses and an elevated balcony that over-looked the lake.

Anyone viewing the structure, whether from the inside or the outside, was unaware that the huge arched waiting room, running east and west over the north end of the train shed, was positioned at right angles to the shed. The room was actually structurally separate from the office building and tower.

Inside, the station's own operating offices and related work spaces took up the first two floors of the office building. A number of railroads made use of the facility. They included the Michigan Central; the Big Four (of the New York Central); the Wisconsin Central; the Chicago, Lake Shore and South Bend (CSS&SB); the Chesapeake & Ohio; and the St. Charles Air Line.

In the late 1800s, the IC was running a number of special trains, such as the "Workingmen's Train," which offered cut-rate tickets to its passengers going to work in the area's mills; the "Washington Park Special," which paused at designated stops to pick up passengers for an evening at the race track; and "Shoppers' Specials," which carried housewives to Downtown Chicago to shop. A daily "Market Train" assured passengers of a fresh supply of meat direct from the largest stockyards in the United States.

The Illinois Central has a powerful identification with Chicago, having brought commuters, passengers and freight to and from the city for more than a century—much of that time with Central Station as the center of all activity. Railroad buffs may recall the old depot fondly, but for future generations, the name Central Station would come to mean a great deal more.

Ward's Historic Stand to Save the Lakefront

Chicago is recognized everywhere as one of the great cities of the world, in part because of its prime location on Lake Michigan. The effort to preserve the city's lakefront has continued through the years as exceptional citizens, such as Aaron Montgomery Ward, placed the public good above selfish comfort. Generations to come may remember Ward as the founder of a catalog-shopping empire and a chain of department stores that have ceased to exist. But Ward deserves to be recognized as one of the city's most important preservationists.

In 1887, he bought property for a building on the west side of Michigan Avenue. Across the street from this site was the then-shabby shoreline area called Lake Park. It took some 20 years and an enormous amount of

(Bottom Left) Creating the retaining wall foundation
(Top Left) Laying up stone on the retaining wall
(Top Right) Depressing the track
(Bottom Right) Trenching for drain pipe

Ward's money to fight construction attempts so the property could become Grant Park.

Between 1890 and 1911, Ward sued the city four times to stop it "from filling the park with public buildings." A provision of Marshall Field's will left $8 million for the creation of a museum on the condition that the city furnish a site, free of cost, within six years of his death. The city wanted that site to be a parcel of Grant Park, but Aaron Montgomery Ward went to court to block all such efforts, being upheld by the court in each instance.

As the owner of two and one-half lots between Washington and Madison Streets, with Michigan Avenue frontage, Ward contended that he owned the public area east of Michigan Avenue and with it a right of private property and the right to keep the area open and unobstructed in order to provide light, air and view to the property owners on the west side of Michigan Avenue. Ward based his contention, according to legal scholars, on a notation on an 1836 subdivision map which designated the area as "public ground, forever to remain vacant of building." The court sided with Ward.

While it was clearly in Ward's own self-interest, this also became the legal precedent to keep the park and lakefront open and free for the people of Chicago for years after Ward had gone. Attacked by the *Chicago Tribune* and city leaders of the day and branded "an obstruc-

tionist," Ward gave what is thought to be the only press interview of his career in order to explain his position. He told the *Tribune*:

> I fought for the people of Chicago, but not for the millionaires. In the district bounded by 22nd Street, Chicago Avenue and Halsted live more than 250,000 persons, mostly poor. The city has a magnificent park and boulevard system of some fifty miles, but the poor man's auto is a shank's mare or at best the streetcars. Here is park frontage on the lake, comparing favorably with the Bay of Naples, which city officials would crowd with buildings, transforming the breathing spot for the poor into a showground for the educated rich. I do not think it is right.
>
> Perhaps I may yet see the public appreciate my efforts. But I doubt it.

When A. Montgomery Ward died in 1913, his contribution to the city was just beginning to be recognized. City leaders noted that if it hadn't been for Ward, Grant Park would be a long line of buildings.

By court order, finally accepting that the area along the lakefront would remain a park, the city turned the property over to the South Park Commission which set about enlarging it. Commissioners arranged for street sweepings and dredgings from the river harbor to be dumped east of the IC tracks, creating 50 new acres of land at no cost to taxpayers. Grass and trees were planted. Sidewalks were constructed. Benches were installed. The state legislature supported the effort by giving the commissioners all submerged lands from Randolph to 12th Streets as far out as the Chicago Harbor line.

The newly beautified location was renamed Grant Park in 1901 in honor of President Ulysses S. Grant, who had lived in Galena.

Even now, the Metropolitan Housing and Planning Council remains dedicated to protecting the lakefront. There has rarely been a year when the Council and citizens have not found themselves battling against lakefront overcommercialization.

America, Chicago and the Railroads in Changing Times

In the years after World War I, the railroad tested steam, diesel, and electric power to replace worn-out engines that had been pushed to their limits by wartime traffic. The war years were boom years for the railroads, and there was increased business through the "Roaring Twenties." But just as the Great Depression took its toll on families and other businesses, the railroad business experienced significant cut-backs and a period of belt-tightening.

In 1940, after 47 years in operation, the Central Station building received a thorough cleaning. Both its common brick and dressed brick were steam washed; sandblasting removed the grime from the structure's stone and granite trim; cracks in the building's stone and mortar were tuck-pointed; and windows were freshly caulked.

By 1945, a renovation was clearly in order. A much-needed drainage system was installed. A new train shed was constructed and new station platforms installed and improved.

Later, beginning in 1962 and throughout the sixties, a number of improvements were made to Central Station's facilities. The great waiting room underwent a modernization of sorts. Its dramatic 45-foot vaulted ceiling was covered by a new lower, flat ceiling. It was 20 feet above the waiting room, with 82 fluorescent light fixtures. Ticket offices were remodeled as well.

Chicago had grown to become a world class city and, throughout its existence, the IC's Central Station was a hub of activity, both commercial and social.

America not only moved its goods by rail, but people had come to regard the trains themselves as having

Various views of Illinois Central development

personalities that reflected the country's life and times. In the 1950s, for example, Central Station had a full complement of trains running to all parts of the system. Many of them were destined to become famous or even regarded by some people as classic and symbolic of the era—The Southern Express (which went to New Orleans), The City of New Orleans (which caught up with and passed the Southern Express at Memphis), The City of Miami, and a train known as the Daylight, that went to St. Louis.

There was The Panama Limited, as well as The Seminole, The Green Diamond, The Land 'O Corn, The Louisiana, The Hawkeye (which went to Sioux City), The Night Diamond and many others.

By 1915 the IC's Weldon Coach Yard (which is still in existence today) was the largest in Chicago, with nine miles of track. Situated immediately south and east of the depot, the Yard experienced a number of operational problems, such as complications in getting power to the trains after the roundhouse was moved nearly two miles as part of an expansion in 1900. It would continue to face major operational challenges through the years. The Weldon Yards, built as a temporary building, became of paramount importance in the year 2000.

Practically every IC train, except express runs, short-distance locals and mail trains, included a diner or some other type of food-service car. A dining car would be switched out of Weldon Coach Yards, stocked with the finest, freshest provisions, and put back into its proper place. As late as 1960, many of the IC's trains still included such holdovers from another era as observation-bar-lounges, club-lounges, cafe-lounges, salon-buffets, tavern-lounge-parlors or observation-lounges, all offering food and beverage service.

Chicago was the very center of activity in an era when railroads were considered a very efficient—even elegant—way to travel.

But times were changing.

In 1952, Central Station launched some 19 trains per day, running 4 of them all the way to New Orleans, 3 to St. Louis via Springfield, 3 along the western lines to Iowa, 1 to Champaign and 6 to Indianapolis or Cincinnati as well as to numerous stops in Florida. On a typical day, the first train would leave the station at 12:20 a.m., the last at 11:50 p.m.

By 1962, only a decade later, the number had declined from 19 trains per day to 11.

By 1968, one-by-one, the railroads operating out of Central Station began reducing luxury services down to a Chicago/Springfield run designated as The Governor's Special. Amtrak discontinued this train in favor of other lines when it took over in May of 1971. By that time, Amtrak had nearly all the long distance passenger services in the United States and had cancelled most of the trains that had been running under other railroad sponsorships.

As of March 6, 1972, all train service from the Central Station had been transferred to Union Station, though the IC's general offices remained at the site.

Without ceremony or fanfare, Central Station closed its doors to the public in 1972.

By early 1974, the once-great Central Station was empty for the first time in 81 years. The property was subsequently demolished, including an annexed building at 1219 South Michigan Avenue. Nothing remains of the launch pad for the fleet of the IC Limiteds. Amtrak trains continued to operate over the IC's main line south of the old station complex well after the Station was gone and Metra purchased the tracks for the regional commuter service.

To business leaders of the era, according to Professor Miller, "urban growth was greatness." The growth of Chicago fostered great economic opportunity, but also created major health and environmental problems: "In moving to meet these problems while continuing to grow, Chicago revealed what would long remain its greatest strengths and weaknesses as a city."

Building on the City's Strengths

The development of the city's lakefront was clearly a critical part of its history. Despite intense political bickering, more than $1 billion went into new landfill on the Lake Michigan shoreline and in construction of recreational and commercial facilities along the water's edge.

Grant Park had been built on land fill east of Michigan Avenue. Cutting through the park, the IC's electrified suburban trains had gone below grade. The Field Museum of Natural History, built in 1919; the Shedd Aquarium (1929) and the Adler Planetarium (1930) were created to form what one historian described as "the largest, oldest and architecturally most impressive 'cultural center'" in the United States." This complex included the Public Library building (built in 1897) to the north and, along the periphery of Grant Park, the Art Institute of Chicago (1893), Orchestra Hall (built in 1904 and permanent home of the Chicago Symphony), the Fine Arts Building (1886) and the Auditorium (1889). At the south end of the park stands Soldier Field, which was built to serve as an all-purpose outdoor stadium.

The Lakefront Ordinance of 1919 was the key to large-scale lakeshore improvement and to the protection

The glamour of rail travel

and preservation of the lakefront. It reflected the agreements made by the IC with the City of Chicago and the South Park Commission, which cleared the way for the public development of the shoreline south of the city's center. The Park Commission had intended to string "a necklace of islands" along the water's edge, according to the Chicago Plan. Except for Northerly Island, which actually became a peninsula, the island concept was never developed.

Visionaries Shape and Mark the City's Lakefront

Chicago became a world-class city, carefully managing its shipping, trading, commercial and financial opportunities. But nearly two centuries ago, its visionaries, acting on the city's behalf, did what no other city in the world had done. Chicago would give its most priceless land, its infinitely valuable shoreline, to the people. The lakefront would be dedicated to pleasure and beauty, not to commerce and industry. Whenever Chicagoans gazed on this spectacular shoreline, they would be as rich as the barons of the Riviera.

Many illustrious names from Chicago's history have been part of the great and ongoing effort to preserve the lakeshore — Daniel Burnham, the architect and city planner; Kate Buckingham whose gift, in memory of her brother Clarence, of a splendid fountain continues to enhance the city's lakefront; Frederick Law Olmsted, the landscape genius who painted with ponds and wooded slopes, creating green lawns and lake views and curbing pass, and designed a superb complex of parks linked by the green midway of park land. In his 1909 *Plan of Chicago*, Burnham wrote:

The lakefront by right, belongs to the people. It affords their one great unobstructed view, stretching away to the horizon, where water and clouds seem to meet. No mountains or high hills enable us to look over broad expanses of the earth's surface; and, perforce we must come even to the margin of the lake for such survey of nature. These views calm thoughts and feelings, and afford escape from the petty things of life. Mere breadth of view, however, is not all. The lake is living water, ever in motion and ever changing in color and in the form of its waves. Across its surface comes the broad pathway of light made by the rising sun; it mirrors the ever-changing forms of the clouds, and is illumined by the glow of the evening sky. Its colors vary with the shadows that play upon it. In every aspect, it is a living thing, delighting man's eye and refreshing his spirit. Not a foot of its shores should be appropriated by individuals to the exclusion of the people. On the contrary, everything possible should be done to enhance its natural beauties, thus fitting it for the part it has to play in the life of the whole city. It should be made so alluring that it will become the fixed habit of the people to seek its restful presence at every opportunity.

Burnham was a large, genial energetic man from New England who was as talented at promotion as he was at architecture. He had the ability to create stirring phrases and the passion to change a city. Burnham said, "Beauty has always paid better than any other commodity."

He is remembered for his eloquent words that touched and inspired even the hardened business leaders of the time. Burnham told them:

Make no little plans. They have no magic to stir man's blood . . . make big plans, aim high and hope and work, remembering that a noble, logical diagram once recorded will never die, but, long after we are gone will be a living thing asserting itself with growing intensity.

Later, he added, "Let your watchword be order and your beacon beauty."

In 1909, Burnham published his Plan for Chicago. The plan did not include the area that is now "Central Station" since he believed there would always be a railroad station.

Today, the 80-plus acres that comprise the Central Station community reflect a total planning effort in which the many architects, designers and the development team of Forest City/Fogelson have created a place that follows the precepts of Burnham combined with the modern needs of today.

The surrounding area has also undergone a transformation from being underdeveloped and neglected to a vibrant, exciting and culturally diverse neighborhood and community.

The IC was, in its own way, a very important and vibrant part of Chicago's history. Now, so many years later, its legacy is reflected in the energy of a community alive with new homes, parks, gardens and cultural connections that have created a bridge from the city's past to its future.

The Story of Central Station

IN APRIL OF 1988 I RECEIVED A TELEPHONE CALL from Larry Mayer, a Chicago real estate broker who had sold property to my company on previous occasions. He wanted to show me what he described as "an unusual real estate listing." Having spent most of my adult life as a developer, I'm always curious to know what others consider an "unusual" piece of real estate.

Mayer explained he had been retained by the Illinois Central Railroad to sell 69 acres of fee and air rights in Chicago's South Loop. The Illinois Central had been a major carrier of both freight and passengers to Chicago, and the property had once been the site of a passenger station and a railroad freight yard. The IC had discontinued that part of its business and sold the tracks to Metra, a regional transportation system.

The railroad station had been demolished for several years and the Illinois Central now wanted to sell both the air rights above the Metra tracks and the fee land so it could generate cash. The IC was highly motivated, as it was in the process of being spun-off from the Whitman Corporation and was planning a public offering of its own.

I had been a real estate developer since 1955 and had enjoyed considerable success with a diverse list of projects. During an earlier period in the 1970s and 1980s, I was the managing general partner in a joint venture with the Norfolk and Western Railroad. We developed a substantial parcel of property the railroad owned in Hammond, Indiana—a development that became known as Briar East, and included a shopping center, an industrial park, a large rental apartment complex, and a number of commercial outpieces.

While Briar East was a 50/50 partnership, I had insisted on having total day-to-day control of the development. This type of arrangement was very unusual for a railroad. It was especially unusual in *this* situation because, in their entire organization, they did not have any individual partners, much less one having the sole right to make decisions of this magnitude. For them to accept this arrangement was a major compliment.

It began an excellent relationship, and the resulting $30 million project was a huge success. Some eight or nine years after we began, I bought out the railroad's interest in Briar East. Years later, I sold the shopping center and apartments on a very favorable basis.

I continued in various aspects of the land, development and construction business.

Public corporations building homes during the 1970s needed to build rapidly. They wanted to buy properties that were all ready to start. I became, in effect, a *lot manufacturer or land manufactuer*—buying land by the acre and selling it by the lot. I also built thousands of rental apartments and houses that I sold for my own account.

I learned a lot about all types real estate—the shopping center business, industrial real estate, office buildings and commercial. We bought a lot of property and would spin of some the pieces to other builders, but I also developed quite a bit myself. We had a management company, construction company and land acquisition team. We had sales and leasing people and were fully engaged in all aspects of the business.

We also did some "adaptive re-use" projects. I bought the Patterson McCormick mansion, which was a Stanford White-designed building on Astor Street in Chicago. Triple-landmarked by the State of Illinois, the City of Chicago *and* the Federal Landmarks Commission, it had fallen into disrepair. The mansion had about 90 rooms. We demolished some of those rooms and reconfigured the building's interior, but we never touched the exterior, except to repair it. We used an architectural historian so that the building, from the outside, looked exactly as it had in its heyday.

I also purchased a rundown building at 867 North Dearborn Street—an old mansion. We restored it, bought the brownstone next to it and put the two buildings together. We connected the buildings plus built another building to create our offices. We were able to create beautiful offices that were very different from those of other people in my business or, I guess, *most* businesses. We also operated differently, including the way we positioned ourselves. Because I had acquired knowledge from doing a wide range of deals, I knew how to do adaptive re-use and commercial, retail, single-family houses and condos, rental apartments, etc. As a result, we did eclectic deals. We would pick the spot and create the use we thought had the best chance for success at that time. Therefore, we moved around more than most other firms that specialized in one or two disciplines.

Larry Mayer was unaware of my earlier involvement with a railroad, but he knew me to be an active developer with a particular interest in land transactions and a history of developing an eclectic list of properties. From his description of the IC property, I wanted to know more.

We drove to the site at 12th Street and Michigan Avenue. As we made our way around the property, I was astounded by the fact that this much land was still available in a city as densely built up as Chicago. The site extended from 12th Street to 21st Street and from Lake Shore Drive to Michigan Avenue. It was bisected by Indiana Avenue, a north/south artery that meandered through the north end of the property.

Though intrigued by both the size and location, I had

serious concerns about the complexity of developing such a challenging site. I decided to discuss the matter with Leonard Schanfield, a senior partner in the law firm of Rosenthal and Schanfield. More than a great attorney and a close friend, I also thought of Leonard as my mentor.

In his office at Wabash and Monroe in Chicago, Schanfield stood looking out his window at the very site I had come to discuss.

He told me how he had often stood at this window, looking at that vast expanse of undeveloped real estate and had always been intrigued by its existence. He strongly urged me to pursue acquisition of the property, arguing that my background in mixed-use development would be a huge advantage and my experience working with the Norfolk and Western made me a good candidate to develop this site.

I had an understanding of how railroad people thought and operated, how they kept their books and what motivated them. Railroad accounting, railroad law and "the railroad approach" are different than those of many other businesses. I thought the experience of having been "accepted" into the railroad fraternity, so to speak, might give me an advantage, both in negotiations for the purchase of the land and, if we were to go forward, in dealing with the IC railroad.

I had to consider the ramifications of such a project. If this development were done well, it would be not only the most important undertaking of my career, but a property so significant in scope that it would have a measurable and lasting effect on the city itself. I was surprised to learn that the IC property had been the only major piece of real estate that had not been planned by the legendary Daniel Burnham, Planner of Chicago.

It seems Burnham had assumed that a railroad yard would forever remain a railroad yard and, therefore, could not be incorporated into his master plan. With all due respect to Daniel Burnham, I was about to try and prove his assumption incorrect and demonstrate that this property was very relevent to many macro changes that could impact the entire city.

—◻—

At a meeting with the IC executives we discussed their asking price, the desired timing and conditions relating to the real estate and a good deal more. The meeting increased my interest in the property, particularly because I felt the asking price was relatively modest. I studied the property further and felt it should be developed for both sale and rental housing of various types and that the air rights should be retained for future use. My prior experience suggested that a commercial shopping center could be located at Roosevelt Road and Michigan Avenue. The overall development held great promise if we could make it all work.

I drew upon some of my previous contacts, most of them from the Chicago suburbs. Jerry Estes was hired to assist in land planning, and we began working with civil engineers and consultants to sketch a preliminary site plan so we could test the densities and possible uses of the property. A review of local zoning ordinances and accumulated relevant data convinced me the property was worth developing. I arranged a second meeting with the IC.

My experiences had taught me how important it was to establish strong credibility in the eyes of the railroad's people. It had been a critical factor in the early stages of our relationship with the Norfolk and Western. I prepared an extensive resume of my experience with Norfolk and Western, as well as a detailed presentation of my other work, together with a long list of references. To further enhance my credibility, I was accompanied by a substantial contingent of experts from The Fogelson Companies. This seemed to impress the IC people, in no small part, I'm convinced, because of the railroad group's "comfort in numbers mentality."

During the weeks that followed, a deal was negotiated between the parties and a contract was executed in 1988. There were many contingencies that would have to be met regarding environmental considerations, soil-bearing capacities, survey and title issues, the securing of zoning approvals from the City of Chicago, as well as approvals of other departments of government, so that a master plan could be put in place and subsequently built out. I was not obligated to take title to the property unless and until these conditions were satisfied within a specified period of time.

The IC property was impacted by several critically important documents, including the Lake Shore Protection Ordinance and the Montgomery Ward Ordinance, both of which held restrictive conditions that affected all properties within proximity of Lake Michigan.

Various Chicago citizens' organizations were actively engaged in the preservation of the parks, the view corridors and the lake. Although ultimate approvals required action by the city Department of Planning, the consent of Alderman Burt Natarus and the City Council, these citizens groups had much to say about this real estate and how it would be developed. I did not fully appreciate at the time how complex these rules would be and to what extent they would affect the future development of the property.

The IC property we were buying was described in rods and chains, rather than in acres or feet. No title insurance existed, only old abstracts. Leonard Schanfield assembled a legal team to track these abstracts and determine the actual legal description of the real estate. The title could then be made perfect as part of the planning and contingency satisfaction for the site. My associates and I were very concerned about the environmental impact of the property having been an active railroad receiving yard. Emissions from the incoming trains could create layers of pollutants that would seriously effect the land. Our research indicated, however, that the trains that used the yard had been primarily steam engines, not diesels, reducing the likelihood of environmental contamination.

In further studying the site, we learned a great deal about not only the property itself, but the role it played in Chicago commerce through the years. Steam engine freight trains would arrive at the rail yard and off-load dry goods and other material. A network of tunnels, constructed under the city, enabled wagons and trucks to transport materials to the great stores on State Street. Marshall Field's, Carson Pirie Scott, Sears Roebuck, Montgomery Ward and other business establishments received much of their merchandise through these tunnels.

The creators of the tunnels could not have foreseen so long ago how these very tunnels would prove to be extremely valuable to the Central Station property. Decades after serving as the delivery route for merchandise, they would be a corridor for fiber optic lines that now provide the property with the city's finest system of fiber optics and electronic highways.

During the contingency satisfaction period, I assembled a good team, all with Chicago experience. The law firm of Trkla, Pettigrew, Allen & Payne was retained as our consultant on tax subsidies and other government programs. Dennis Hardin, first assigned as Trkla's representative on the project, was later hired by Central Station to be part of the Central Station development team.

It was during this time period that I learned Leonard Schanfield was in the early stages of cancer. I was deeply affected by this on both a personal and a business level. He was, above all else, my closest friend and mentor. He had been the best man at my wedding and my kids thought of him as "Uncle Leonard." He had also been instrumental in encouraging me to pursue what we both knew would be a pivotal development in the future of our great city, as well as the most significant project of my own career. He was closely involved in all aspects of strategy, planning and work that went well beyond the legal aspects of this monumental development. I wanted to spend as much time with him as possible during what would turn out to be the last brief years of his extraordinary life. He was the brightest man I had ever known.

I also relied heavily on an extremely gifted and competent young woman named Billie Jo Spathies. I had hired her 12 years earlier to work in our accounting department when she was just 21 years old. B.J. had been with me through recession, cutbacks and reorganizations, working her way up to Executive Vice President and junior partner. She eventually became President of the Fogelson Companies, before starting her own firm. (B.J. is now a respected developer in Chicago real estate in the company I helped her name, BEJCO.) She was especially strong in administrative matters and in dealing with accounting and finances.

It was Leonard Schanfield who first suggested I meet with Albert B. Ratner, the chairman of Forest City Enterprises, a Cleveland-based company that is highly regarded in developing urban real estate throughout the United States. Ratner himself is a huge player on the national scene in all forms of real estate activity and a respected figure with impeccable credentials in the industry

Ratner already had a significant connection to Chicago. After the tragic loss of his first wife in an automobile accident, he married Audrey Pritzker, the former wife of Robert Pritzker, co-owner of the Pritzker Corporations. Audrey had lived in Chicago prior to her marriage to Albert Ratner. Her personal attorney was Leonard Schanfield. Her accountant was Paul Anglin, of Deloitte & Touche, who was coincidentally my own personal accountant and a very close confidante.

Separately, Schanfield and Anglin had both contacted Al Ratner and suggested that he and I should meet regarding the IC project. Schanfield advised me to secure a "deep pocket" investor since the financial "carry" costs and the complexity of the development would require larger capital and organizational commitments than the Fogelson group had at the time.

Albert Ratner and I connected with one another immediately. We were two people who were *multi-lingual* in a rather unique sense. By that I mean, although his company was much bigger and more successful than mine, there was no one in his company who was really *multi-deal-lingual*. And now he meets this other guy who is *multi-deal-lingual* and we start talking about getting involved in a multi-use property. The fact that we could both speak the same language and flow from property type to property type was the start of what we called "The Jerry and Albert Show." We just liked each other and sparked off each other.

As we toured the IC property, his interest was apparent. He suggested I fly back to Cleveland with him that very same day on his corporate jet to continue our discussion. He also wanted me to see a development the Forest City organization had under construction, a major mixed-use development in downtown Cleveland—and it was being constructed over railroad tracks. Ratner was eager to show me some of the work his company was doing and tied in the railroad aspect with the Chicago site.

We met again a week later in Chicago, discussed a deal and shook hands. That handshake began a relationship that resulted in the development of some 80 acres of property, involving billions of dollars in construction. It would also have far reaching consequences, affecting the future development of the entire Near South area of Chicago, as well as Soldier Field and what would become known as the Museum Campus (the Adler Planetarium, Field Museum and Shedd Aquarium, and much more).

Ratner's experience was in large-scale mixed-use development. Forest City Enterprises develops, acquires, owns and manages commercial, residential, hotel and retail properties in 21 states. They are one of the big players in American real estate.

It was Albert's suggestion that we arrange a competition in which architects and land planners would evaluate the preliminary land plan that had been suggested by my team. This competition resulted in our retaining Stanton Ecksted of Ehrenkrantz & Ecksted from New York as the master planner for the site.

Al Ratner felt the best direction to take the development was toward the creation of large "back office buildings" similar to his successful developments in New York. Ecksted's plans encompassed a development that consisted of 18 million square feet with a substantial portion of the property to be built over a deck. That deck would conceal a network of roads for deliveries, utilities and other uses, as well as be the structure for parking. The emphasis of the development plan was shifted from residential to commercial.

In 1989, we retained a number of experts and consultants to study the retail possibilities of the site as well as the potential for residential, office, commercial and institutional use. We kept these consultants apart from each other so when we collected all the information, we could better assess what the highest and best use of the property would be. Concurrently, the design team, led by Stan Ecksted, produced massive drawings, traffic studies and parking studies for the master plan. Dozens of companies worked on the massive planning exercise.

When the studies were completed and reviewed, I was still convinced the highest and best use for the site was condominium residential. Ratner believed just as strongly that back office space would be a better use for this location and would be more financially lucrative.

We resolved the land plan by creating three distinct planning areas. The north end of the site, from 12th Street (Roosevelt Road) to 14th Street, was designed primarily for commercial, hotel and office use; the area from 14th Street to 16th Street was designated as a residential area; and 16th Street to 20th Street would be for convention-related, residential and institutional use. The plan was unfolding in a more dramatic form than I had expected and looked to offer even greater potential. I was really excited.

The Commissioner of Planning for the City of Chicago at that time was David Mosena, a man with an excellent education in urban planning and a great deal of sophistication in that area. Mosena was supportive of the planning effort, but determined that, because of the high visibility of this property and its potential impact on the entire area, the property would have to be done as a "master plan." He required us to create what came to be known as *The Central Station Guidelines*. This 90-page book analyzed and dealt with every possible aspect of the property, including view corridors, park areas, building heights, density and uses. The feeling was that a "guideline plan" would enable the long-term develop-

ment to have flexibility within agreed-upon parameters; we could adjust uses and densities if we stayed within the guidelines and received approvals from the city. The guidelines also set up a procedure for multiple reviews for each specific step. It was and still is the toughest Planned Unit Development in the city. We have spent hundreds of hours with the Department of Planning and continue to do so.

The Central Station Partnership put the law firm of Daley & George on retainer to assist us in what we understood would be a long series of approvals and interactions with government and others due to the complexity of the Planned Unit Development. Leonard Schanfield had played an integral part in so much of what we had done to date, from overseeing all the legal matters involved in the purchase of the IC property and title clearance to providing valuable advice and counsel on most of the major business decisions. Now Jack George, being a land use attorney, would guide us through the plan development process and assure that we were in total conformance with all city ordinances and zoning restrictions as each phase of Central Station got underway.

Jack George became a key member of the Central Station team. He is thorough and extremely knowledgeable in matters of law. Jack and I, along with others on the Central Station team, worked closely in preparing the *Guidelines* and presentations for various planning groups and the City Council. We became good friends and have worked closely ever since.

As captain of the team, I was completely absorbed in the development. I spoke frequently with Albert Ratner and he became a "sounding board" for countless ideas, but it was up to me to shepherd the plan into the finished product. This was an especially challenging task because of both the enormity of the development and the scrutiny to which it would be subjected. I had full authority to bind the project, just as I'd had in the Norfolk and Western days.

Immersing ourselves in the project and the area, my wife Georgia and I visited the Museum Campus. We went first to the Field Museum of Natural History, America's largest institution of its kind, and were surprised to find that nowhere in the museum bookstore was there information on how this amazing and important institution had come into being, much less anything describing its relationship to the other museums that were in such close proximity. Similarly, neither the Adler Planetarium nor the Shedd Aquarium (later to be known as the Shedd Oceanarium) could offer any such historical information.

Georgia's background had been in market research.

She had owned and operated a successful company of her own, Georgia Bender Research, and was recognized throughout the United States for her expertise. When I bought the Central Station property, she agreed to take on special projects that benefitted the development, working mostly behind the scenes. She not only had experience and the required insatiable interest in learning, but the knowledge of how to thoroughly research the history of these three very significant institutions and the entire area.

The Field Museum, 11 acres devoted to anthropology, botany, geology and zoology, was built in part with an $8 million gift from the will of Marshall Field. The Shedd Aquarium, established in 1930, was made possible by a $3 million donation from John G. Shedd, who at the time was president of Marshall Field & Company. The Adler Planetarium and Astronomical Museum, also opened in 1930, was the first planetarium to be built in America. It was made possible by a donation from Chicago philanthropist Max Adler. At the northern end of Northerly Island, the 12-sided structure designed by Ernest A. Grunsfeld, Jr., won the 1930 Gold Medal from the Chicago Chapter of the American Institute of Architects. These three world-class institutions provide the city with cultural richness, enhanced by the fact that they share a common area, the Museum Campus.

Georgia spent weeks at the Historical Society, reviewing thousands of old papers and combing the archives of the *Chicago Tribune*, securing such information as was available. Ultimately, we were able to get the directors of the three institutions talking to one another on mutually important issues. Each had perceived the other as a competitor of sorts, going after the same targeted market. They had not worked together to attract more visitors and thereby *expand* their total market. Now there was an opportunity for them to help define how the former IC property could "fill the hole in the donut," creating easier access to the museums and enabling the three to become *one central island of culture*.

The result of Georgia's efforts was what we described at the time as a "talking document" that helped us to understand how the museum area came into being and provided us with greater insight as to the implications and the interfacing between the museum property and our development parcel. We learned, quite interestingly, that the area designated as the Museum Campus and the Illinois Central property were closely linked throughout the history of Chicago. Ours was, after all, the property that had been created when the city, in permitting the Illinois Central Railroad the right to lay tracks leading into Chicago, traded land to the IC in exchange for the railroad's promise to construct a barrier that would protect the shoreline and lakefront homes from further land erosion and storm damage. Since the land the city traded was under water at the time, the result of erosion of the shoreline, the tracks were built on trestles in Lake Michigan and the city's subsequent landfill project created the land that ultimately joined the museum sites, parks and Central Station property.

The Selection of a Name

A project of this magnitude needed a name, and we realized that whatever name we gave it would have major implications on a number of levels for many years to come.

Georgia had uncovered and collected a great deal of information about the Central Station, together with photographs and considerable historical data. After much discussion, our team concluded that "Central Station" would be the ideal name for the development.

At the time, most people assumed (and continue to believe) the property's name comes from there having once been the actual Central Station depot on the site, back when it was the center of railroad activity. That makes a good story, but it wasn't how we reached our decision.

I wanted the name because of the word "central." I

thought Central Station would help differentiate the property's location and position us as a more *central location* within the city—not just as a part of the Near South Side. Time has proven the name to be a good choice.

Mayor Daley and His City

Richard M. Daley was elected mayor of Chicago in 1989, and we began working very closely with him on Central Station from the very beginning. For a property of this size—and because it was the only remaining piece of undeveloped property along Lake Shore Drive—every decision had to be cleared by the mayor. We have worked with many planning commissioners and countless others, but all major decisions in connection with the development went directly to Mayor Daley.

In 1999, when we revised the plan for everything north of 14th Street, it was Mayor Daley who requested we make a gift of all the land from Roosevelt Road to 14th Street to extend the park and cover the tracks. We agreed, and a very substantial parcel of land was given to the city. Plans were announced in 2001 to move the site of the city's very popular "Taste of Chicago" event to land given to the city by the Central Station Develop-

ment Corporation. We found working with the mayor to be a very positive experience. He is an astute, focused and fair-minded man who brought a great deal of insight to our deliberations and contributed much to the vision of Central Station.

The South Side of Chicago

Chicago is a city where the historic rivalry between the north and south sides of town is widely known and accepted. It is a source of good-natured fun and neighborhood pride. In 1989, the public considered being "south" in Chicago a negative in real estate terms. Most of the area south of the Loop was in extreme disrepair, marked by wide areas of rundown buildings and underutilized property. The South Side was not the "fashionable" part of town, a situation that did not serve the interests of real estate brokers and developers any more than it helped the residents of the community. That had not always been the case.

When the Great Chicago Fire destroyed much of the city in 1871, the blaze began at approximately 12th Street and spread north. More than 17,000 buildings were destroyed. Fire raged across some 2,100 acres with about 70 percent of the damage hitting the city's north side.

Virtually all of the major building and development activity in Chicago during the past hundred years has been north of the river and in the Loop area, essentially rebuilding or replacing what was destroyed. With relatively little damage south of 12th Street and because the emphasis was on restoring what was north of the river, the city's Near South Side fell into a state of disrepair that went largely ignored for years.

The southernmost location of the "Near South Side" was 22nd Street, also known as Cermak Road. Anton Cermak, the mayor of Chicago from 1931 to 1933, was killed by an assassin whose actual target had been President Franklin Roosevelt. Following Mayor Cermak's death, 22nd Street was renamed to honor him. At the insistence of Colonel Robert McCormick, the influential publisher of the powerful *Chicago Tribune*, McCormick Place had been built east of Lake Shore Drive and on the lake, at Cermak Road.

Other than the museums, McCormick Place was the only building ever built on the lakefront. McCormick Place 2, located west of Lake Shore Drive and on the north side of Cermak Road, was completed in 1986. These two buildings, together with the McCormick Inn Hotel, represented the end of the Near South Side.

Beginning a new development and making it a success is a highly involved, hugely expensive, and challenging endeavor under the best of circumstances. In the case of Central Station, we had all the usual challenges *plus* perceptions about safety, diversity and quality of life in an area regarded as "unfashionable." We chose to meet the challenges head-on.

Partners for Progress

Albert Ratner described to me a technique he had used successfully in other large-scale urban developments. He called it a "Partnership for Progress." He suggested I visit each of the major "stakeholders" in the area to determine what they wanted done with the property and bring them together as a support group for what would eventually be our zoning effort. Ratner also suggested that Joseph Pigott, a former educator and a key player in the development of the Cleveland Clinic, be brought in as a consultant to assist in this exploratory effort with the "stakeholders." Joe was able to effectively communicate with institutional leaders of all types.

Over the next six months or so, Pigott and I held a number of meetings with representatives of the Hilton

Hotel, the Field Museum, Adler Planetarium, Shedd Oceanarium, McCormick Place, Mercy Hospital, Michael Reese Hospital, the Near South Side Planning Board, the Park District, the Donnelley Corporation and the colleges and universities located in the area: Roosevelt University, Columbia College, DePaul University, and the Spertus Institute and other influential property owners.

South of 22nd Street is Chicago's South Side, and its population was mainly African-American. The Michael Reese Hospital Campus, a predominantly Jewish hospital, and the Mercy Hospital Campus, a Catholic hospital operated by the Sisters of Mercy Healthcare Corporation, were important fixtures in this area.

The president of Mercy Hospital was Sister Sheila, a charismatic and highly intelligent woman of great spirit. She and I established an immediate rapport and came to know each other well. My respect for her only grew as time went by. Sister Sheila continued to play an important role, as did Mercy Hospital, in the "Partners for Progress." This was the medical facility of Chicago's Mayor Richard Daley and his family and was held in high regard by much of the city's Irish population—as well its *political* population. A portion of the hospital was named to honor Illinois' highly influential former Congressman Dan Rostenkowski.

The various meetings with the stakeholders enabled the Central Station team to assess which elements of our proposal were of particular interest to the community. This information was then given to our planners so the revised plan would reflect the major concerns of residents and businesses in the area, as well as those of the city itself.

Roosevelt Road and Other Major Features

What emerged as one of the single most important considerations was the need to provide an extension of Roosevelt Road. The only existing access routes to the all-important Lake Shore Drive were at Cermak Road, passing through the McCormick Place complex with its heavy traffic (and conflicting agendas), and at Balboa Drive, located at 9th Street, just north of the Hilton Hotel. Not only was access to Lake Shore Drive difficult, but getting to the Museum Campus was extremely challenging as well.

For years, the city had tried unsuccessfully to work out an easement or program of some kind with the Illinois Central to extend Roosevelt Road across its property.

Representatives of the City of Chicago were eager to take advantage of an opportunity to extend Roosevelt Road as a part of the planning of the Central Station property.

Other major considerations in the planning included providing view corridors at various locations to create a visible connection between the lakefront, Michigan Avenue and Indiana Avenue, open spaces and green space and building heights.

Indiana Avenue was a major four-lane street until it intersected within the Central Station area at 14th Street. Then the street narrowed from four lanes to two lanes and meandered through the property, eventually intersecting at Roosevelt Road. Therefore, another major aspect of the planning was to extend Indiana Avenue at a four-lane width up to what would be the extension of Roosevelt Road.

As our plan began to take shape, I was able to gain the support of the various stakeholders in the area through our one-on-one meetings and the periodic group meetings where various planning aspects were discussed and embraced by the "Partners for Progress."

Theodore L. Gross was the President of Roosevelt University during this period, having arrived in Chicago at about the same time the Central Station plan was being created. As a dynamic and aggressive leader, he enthusiastically supported the plan, as did

John Duff, then-President of Columbia College, and Father Richards of DePaul University. The support of Father Richards was particularly important to us because of the increasing importance of DePaul in the area, and the high degree of respect he had achieved in his many years in a position of leadership at the university and in the city.

(Some years later, I became a Trustee at Roosevelt University and, in the year 2000, I led and helped fund an effort to create The Chicago School of Real Estate at Roosevelt University. The hope is that the school's undergraduate and graduate programs will be among the premier real estate schools in the United States, on a par with The University of Wisconsin, The Wharton School and The University of Denver, among other fine institutions that offer such programs. There is now a Gerald W. Fogelson endowed chair at the Chicago School of Real Estate.)

Central Station and The Chicago Park District

The museums and Soldier Field are all owned by the Chicago Park District, the largest employer in the city. The Chicago Park District leases the buildings to the museums and has a considerable voice in matters such as the fees they can charge, their policies and any number of other issues. The largest source of revenue for the Park District is Soldier Field and the parking fees from events staged there—primarily the Chicago Bears football games.

In 1989, the most influential member of the Park District board was Walter Netsch, a retired architect who had been a partner in Skidmore, Owings & Merrill. Netsch was extremely interested in the Central Station development and its impact on Park District property. A man of strong opinions, he lived on Astor Street and knew me from my work in restoring the Patterson McCormick mansion, which was located almost adjacent to his home.

The Patterson McCormick mansion, as noted earlier, had been designed by Stanford White and built originally for Cissy Patterson, the wife of the founder of the *Chicago Tribune*. It was later occupied by Cyrus McCormick III. This landmark building, at Burton and Astor, stood empty for years. It had special significance to Netsch, not only because of its immediate proximity to his own home, but because of his architectural acuity. When I acquired the property, restored it and converted it to nine luxurious condominiums, I received support from the residents of Chicago's Gold Coast and, especially, from Walter Netsch.

The Park District and the museums were extremely interested in changing the traffic pattern of Lake Shore Drive which, at that time, had a northbound lane that separated the Field Museum from the Adler Planetarium and the Shedd Oceanarium, and a southbound lane that ran adjacent to the Central Station property.

The museum people wanted to eliminate the northbound lane and expand the southbound lane for traffic in both directions, thus creating a unified campus without a high-traffic road bisecting the buildings. To accomplish this, they needed the cooperation of Metra, the owner of the tracks west of Lake Shore Drive, and of Central Station, the owner of the air rights and the fee property over and adjacent to the tracks. Although the degree of cooperation needed wasn't known at that time, the planning for rerouting Lake Shore Drive was being discussed and was considered as part of the *Guidelines*.

Approval of Our Plan

The plan submitted to the Chicago Plan Commission received the enthusiastic support of all of the members of the "Partners for Progress" and a favorable recommendation from Commissioner David Mosena and his staff.

There was no opposition to the proposed development in part because of the efforts within the community that had preceded the submission. In fact, virtually no one living in the area had a reason to object. On March 1, 1990, the Commission approved and adopted the *Central Station Development Guidelines.*

After the vote, Commission chairman Rueben L. Hedlund described this as the most important piece of planning in the recent history of Chicago, saying that it finally completed the Daniel Burnham Plan.

With the approval of the Chicago Plan Commission and the City Council, Central Station was a major step closer to becoming reality. But there was still so much to do.

Land Financing

Several banks in Chicago were approached and refused to lend on the property without significant guarantees. Therefore, in order to finance the property, we approached the Hokkaido Takushoku Bank, a large Japanese bank which had been involved in several earlier deals with Forest City. Hokkaido maintained a branch office in Chicago, but all major decisions were made in Tokyo.

Forest City's in-house mortgage department was headed by Bob O'Brien, who was assisted by LeAnn Simonetti. After they had negotiated a commitment acceptable to the bank and to our partnership, a long process of evaluation, appraisal and analysis was conducted by the bank at our expense. This included a comprehensive appraisal employing a methodology only used on large projectsto determine the present value of the property.

Getting Title to the Property

In June 1989, a formal closing took place and the Illinois Central Railroad deeded the property to the Central Station Limited Partnership. The City Council had affirmed the zoning recommendation from the Planning Department and contingencies had been satisfied.

When the sale was final, after the negotiating, planning, working and reworking of the numbers, we officially became the owners of the site of the most ambitious undertaking of my career. Leonard Schanfield, B.J. Spathies, Georgia and I brought a bottle of champagne and drove to the property over rocks, stone and rubble.We got out of the car, sat down in the middle of the property and, with great flair and undisguised excitement, toasted Central Station.

Groundbreaking ceremony for Central Station. From left to right: Albert Ratner, Audrey Ratner, Mayor Richard M. Daley, Georgia Fogelson, and Gerald W. Fogelson.

But as the infrastructure work got underway, the national economy—and the real estate market—went into decline. Interest rates increased. The economy was in a malaise.Very few buildings of any kind were being built in Chicago, and certainly no high-rise buildings.

1304 S. Indiana Avenue

During this same time period, Albert Ratner and I decided to purchase an adjacent property not owned by the Illinois Central, at 1304 S. Indiana Avenue. The four-acre site was located on the west side of where Indiana Avenue would be reconstructed by the partnership. That meant the property would be vastly improved as a result of the newly constructed Indiana Avenue. We demolished the building that occupied the land, and it is now the site of *Museum Park* townhomes and *Museum Park Lofts*.

Tom Small, a civil engineer and construction manager, had joined The Fogelson Companies several years before to administer land development and land planning in our suburban developments. He was assigned to negotiate the prices and administer the installation of needed improvements at Central Station.

Storm and sanitary sewer lines were run east from the Chicago River to the property benefiting not only this property, but others, including the museums. The construction of Indiana Avenue as a four-lane modern street with a wide median to accommodate the planned light rail circulator also benefited the community.

Extending through Central Station was a huge concrete viaduct that had supported railroad tracks. The construction team, which Tom Small also led, demolished this viaduct and moved a heavy crushing machine onto the site so concrete material could be ground right there rather than carried away. This material was then used as road bed for the new streets.

The Start of Residential Construction

The Central Station Partnership had succeeded in the zoning, the tax increment financing (TIF), the acquisition and the financing. However, there was no market for back office, mid-rise or high-rise residential or commercial space. Albert Ratner and I decided we needed to create "a sense of place."

We knew that one of our first major challenges would be to overcome the old images and perceptions of the Near South Side. We had to counter the very strong impression, which seemed to be generally held, that people would not want to live in this area. We made a calculated decision to take a significant piece of fee property, zoned for mid-rise and high-rise buildings, and develop townhomes and low-rise condominiums instead. Our reasoning was that if we built a very attractive development and it was successful, we could affirm the desirability and the livability of the location.

We talked with a number of builders before finally selecting Daniel McLean of MCL Companies, known for the Dearborn Park South development, just south of Roosevelt Road and east of the river.

I had become acquainted with John Melk, one of the original group of people who formed the enormously successful Waste Management Corporation. John became unhappy with the corporate bureaucracy and decided to take an early retirement. About the same time, the co-founder of the company, Wayne Huizenga, and the principal financial officer, Donald Flynn, also retired from Waste Management, leaving control of the company in the hands of another co-founder, Dean Buntrock.

Melk, during his retirement, visited a small operation in Texas. It was known as Blockbuster Video. He convinced Huizenga to run the company with Flynn managing the financial operation. The three men then purchased the small Blockbuster Video chain and, within a few years, it had become one of the largest, fastest-growing businesses, with thousands of stores around the world. John Melk asked me to spend some time with his son Daniel, who wanted to move in a direction other than working in the Blockbuster Video operation.

After getting to know Dan Melk, I recommended that he go to work for MCL so he could learn the construction business. He was hired by Dan McLean on the provision that John Melk would become a money partner in the first two phases of housing at Central Station. The arrangement seemed to give everyone what they needed at the time. A partnership was formed that consisted of Melk, Central Station, and MCL each with a one-third interest.

Harbor Square and Park Row

My wife Georgia named the first two sections of Central Station, using historic names that had some connection to the development. The first condominiums were called Harbor Square, because that part of the development was built on land that had once been part of the lake harbor. The three-story buildings were "over and under"—meaning that the first level was a flat and above it a duplex. Harbor Square was built with one-car garages at the corner of 15th Street and Indiana Avenue. The architect for the project was Roy Cruse & Associates.

We also built Park Row, a development consisting of large townhomes with four living levels, designed by Patrick Fitzgerald of Fitzgerald & Associates, another well known Chicago architectural firm. The name recalled the historic Chicago street that had once been home to Potter and Bertha Palmer, and other socialites of the 19th century.

A large marketing and sales trailer was constructed on the southeast corner of Roosevelt Road and Michigan Avenue. Kenneth Riha, of Riha Design Group, had developed an expertise in creating large temporary trailers that could be placed on sites and function as both sales and administrative offices. The Central Station offices were six trailers, hooked together to create a build-ing with 4,000 square feet of space elaborately fitted with all we needed to market the condominiums and townhomes. Since no actual models were available, scale models were constructed and luxurious but tasteful displays showed the benefits of living in the area. Heavy advertising in the *Chicago Tribune* and elsewhere resulted in significant traffic and strong sales for both Harbor Square and Park Row.

The area attracted a diverse combination of people, including African-Americans, Asians, some who had lived south of the city in communities such as Beverly and Oak Lawn, and an eclectic smattering of people from other parts of the Chicago area. Prices were considered high for this location. Units were very carefully designed to reflect the Prairie style of architecture identified with the area.

The Central Station team constructed Prairie Avenue (a street name with considerable recognition in Chicago) so the development could proceed. This was also built under the supervision of Tom Small. Contemporaneously, work had begun on the all-important Roosevelt Road extension, linking Michigan Avenue to Lake Shore Drive.

We were ecstatic with the success of the townhome and condominium development. Central Station had created a significant stir in Chicago. We believed we had gone a long way toward proving our contention that this was the right kind of development at exactly the right location to help take Chicago into the new century. But there was more to come.

Early in the sales program, we learned the Mayor of Chicago, Richard M. Daley, and his wife Maggie were interested in purchasing a townhome at Park Row and moving with their family to Central Station. The Daleys had lived in the city's Bridgeport area for many years. They were now considering moving closer into the city, while still remaining south.

I arranged for the Mayor and Mrs. Daley to meet with McLean and, very quietly, a contract was entered into at the normal price and under normal conditions. No announcement was made of the purchase, but the press soon learned the mayor had purchased a home at Central Station and word spread quickly throughout the city.

This was more than good publicity for the development. With Central Station known as the area where the mayor lived, many people would consider it the safest part of the city.

The partnership was, of course, delighted to receive the benefits of such positive advertising and public relations news. Sales continued to increase as construction progressed.

The Commercial Component

The Roosevelt Road Bridge construction was going well. Al Ratner and I now believed we would finally be able to attract people to the property who could view the site from the Roosevelt Road bridge. In order to pursue the sale and/or development of commercial and other properties, an elaborate "Central Station" room had been created at our offices at 867 North Dearborn. Scale models were constructed; audio visual presentations were created; graphs, maps and site plans were displayed, all in a high-quality environment that had been carefully designed to create the right atmosphere. But despite the lovely presentation center—even with the Roosevelt Road bridge under construction—we were unable to find any real prospects interested in buying and/or developing any of the site for commercial or office use.

As the recessionary times continued, we became increasingly concerned about the ongoing financial burden of the debt on the property and the significant real estate taxes, since title had passed from railroad ownership to our ownership. There were other expenses, such as the interest on our loan, the accrued interest on our equity and operational costs. Forest City was funding more than it had originally anticipated and I was working non-stop.

We knew the right high-profile commercial connection could be the catalyst to carry us forward.

At about that time, I received a phone call from a Soviet-American citizen who said he was working on behalf of the Soviet Union to find a building in the United States for the purpose of creating a center for culture, trade and commerce. After some discussion—and knowing it was a long-shot—we made a presentation for what was to be known as the Soviet-American Trade Culture and Commerce Building.

The Central Station team had presentation documents prepared in both Russian and English and secured the endorsement of the Governor of Illinois at the time, James R. Thompson, as well as the endorsement of Mayor Daley. We then submitted our proposal to Mikhail Gorbachov, then-leader of the Soviet Union, through the Soviet team.

The Soviet delegation made several trips to Chicago. I retained Tom Miner, who was head of the Mid-America Foreign Relations Council in Chicago and a man with a reputation as an international "deal maker." Miner became our consultant and assisted us in our attempts to understand and work through the bureaucratic Soviet system. The Soviet team was headed by Yuri Platinov, Head of Architecture for the Soviet Union. Platinov was closely connected with the political leadership in Moscow, as well as with businessmen from the Russian State of Georgia. His efforts and the hard currency of the Georgians enabled our proposed development to proceed, albeit at a slow pace.

One of the biggest problems we encountered in dealing with the Soviets was getting them to free up "hard currency." Hard currency was difficult to come by in their ruble-based, inflationary economy pummeled by scarcities of goods and the myriad of economic failures. Regardless, we remained moderately optimistic, and the parties entered into an agreement to create the building using Soviet architects and the American architectural firm of Solomon, Cordwell & Buenz of Chicago.

Ultimately, the protocol agreements (similar to a letter of intent) were signed. A short time later, due to Gorbachov's changes in perestroika—the system of reforms—the Soviet Union ceased to exist. Boris Yeltsin came into power as the President of Russia. Platinov and his team were highly placed within the Yeltsin power structure, as they had been with Gorbachov, and they were able to switch the building from a Soviet-American venture to a Russian-American venture and to secure the approval of the newly elected President Yeltsin.

The Russian team insisted we travel to Moscow to meet President Yeltsin and appropriate dignitaries to re-sign the protocol agreement in their country. In June of

1991, Tom Miner accompanied my wife Georgia and me on a trip to Moscow.

We considered ourselves fairly well-travelled, but we were not prepared for what we were to encounter. Upon our arrival in Moscow, we were shocked at the deteriorated condition of the country overall and the absence of merchandise of any kind in the stores or shops. The buildings were run down, weeds were everywhere and it all looked shabby. We had one of the few Lincoln stretch limos in the entire country; we stayed at the Astor Hotel and were treated like royalty by the Russian government; however, it was abundantly clear that what had been viewed from America as "the evil empire" looked very much like Gary, Indiana, on a gray day.

Yuri Platinov, who with his wife had visited our home in the United States about six months earlier, had organized a series of meetings with various Russian dignitaries that took up the next several days. The purpose of the proposed building at Central Station, the type of materials that would be used in its construction and any number of other details, as well as the importance the building might have as a symbol of the cooperative efforts between the two countries were the subjects of the meetings. If this building could be built at Central Station with the high visibility of our location, on the lake

and by the museums, it would stand as a tangible connection between the United States and Russia.

The sessions began with the architectural groups and later expanded to include a group of Russian officials. These meetings were held around long tables where Tom Miner, Georgia and I, along with two translators, sat on one side, while approximately 15 people sat across from us on "the Russian side." We created a number of drawings and sketches and discussed how the building we envisioned could be developed. We later met with the Deputy Mayor of Moscow and numerous other VIPs, including government officials officed in what had once been the feared Politburo.

Almost every night of our stay in Russia, there was a dinner or event that seemed to have ceremonial overtones. A special reception was to be held in our honor to celebrate the signing of the agreement.

Later, as we dressed for dinner, I asked Georgia to wear her finest jewelry. I was determined that for our special dinner we were going to leave our Russian friends with a favorable impression of American developers in a party atmosphere.

The limo drove us to our destination—a ride we thought would never end. The car snaked endlessly through areas that resembled abandoned public housing developments. Weeds reached halfway to the sky. After an hour, we stepped from the car and were led along weed-covered stepping stones to a rusty Quonset hut that was not visible from the street. Inside, the walls were magnificent; the carpets were some of the finest I have ever seen; waiters walked about with trays of French champagne and pate; the bars were equipped with every imaginable liquor. Women were dressed in designer fashions worthy of a Parisian salon. Accordingly, we were treated like royalty in a palace atmosphere. We realized they did not want people to see the abundance they had while the country was in a time of shortages and despair.

Some of the country's more prominent officials and dignitaries were in attendance. Georgia and I were asked our opinions of the Bolshoi, and we answered that it was much like the building we were in: On the outside, a look of "benign neglect," but inside, it was glorious, magnificent, its rich tradition on display.

We were lead through a beaded curtain to a room with long dinner tables, where we were seated at the head table as the guests of honor. On each table, in front of every *couple*, were bottles of French champagne, Russian champagne, vodka and the dreadful mineral water that had found its way from the meeting rooms. The tables also held huge mounds of fresh fruits, vegetables and caviar. Numerous toasts were of-fered all around. Every man in the room stood to make a toast. I was getting very woozy.

After a gala evening, on the ride back to our hotel, Georgia and I wondered if this deal would ever happen since their thinking about business and architecture was totally different from ours. By the time we prepared to return home, I was doubtful the Russians would be able to come up with the money needed for their share of the venture. Further, we could not get a clear sense of what they actually had to export that would be of interest to American buyers. They were clearly more an importer of goods and services than an exporter, so the program they had originally proposed did not work.

There were flurries of faxes from Russia to the U.S. Communication was difficult. With the Russian economy extremely stressed and so little hard currency available, it was becoming increasingly apparent that this ambitious and well-intentioned project would very likely never get underway. The Russians eventually came up with some hard currency for a feasibility study and we tried to see if it could work. But the challenges were too great, so, after months of negotiations, we agreed to drop the plan. Our partnership was richer for the experience, but was no closer to a solution to addressing the needs of the commercial component of the Central Station plan.

The World Trade Center Concept

In our search for the right commercial component for the development, we evolved a more general concept of a World Trade Center at Central Station, as opposed to simply the offices of individual foreign companies. We learned from talking with a lot of people that the best world trade centers were in Asia—Osaka was building, Seoul, Korea and Taiwan were established. We visited them to see if that could be an appropriate direction for Central Station. After meeting with a variety of trade center officials and business people, we concluded that such a center was not viable for Central Station. To be successful, a World Trade Center had to be underwritten by the government. Furthermore, such centers worked better in countries that were importers.

Exploring The University of Chicago

Much closer to home, the University of Chicago had decided to build a new business school. A request for pro-posals was issued, and we decided to compete for this building in the hope that the University of Chicago's decision-makers would look favorably on our South Loop location, closer to the university's main campus, and regard this building as an effort to establish a new and truly vital area within the city.

We prepared plans sufficient in scope so costs could be estimated, and we supported the proposal with an elaborate presentation to the University's representatives. Ultimately, the University of Chicago decided to build its new facility north of the Chicago River in an area closer to Michigan Avenue and with better transportation to the Northwestern Train Station. The decision was driven by the University's studies that showed its students for evening and weekend classes were from the suburbs and should have an easier and shorter route between the new facility and commuter trains. Therefore, in this instance, as with so many other real estate transactions that came before, it was a matter of "location, location, location."

Senior Suites

We had purchased an additional piece of property that was not a part of the original IC property—a parking lot at the southwest corner of 14th Street and Indiana Avenue. At first, the plan was to build townhomes across the street from the MCL townhomes, possibly at a lower price point. However, William B. Kaplan, chairman of Senior Lifestyle Corporation, was seeking a location to build a subsidized senior apartment complex. Mayor Daley had specifically indicated he wanted senior housing in this area. Known as Senior Suites, these buildings typically from 80 to 100 units, are designed for retired people with limited incomes, usually from pensions or retirement programs.

These buildings had a special real estate tax rate. While they did not offer full services, the facilities had a menu of services from which people could select. As longtime friends, Bill Kaplan and I were able to quickly reach an agreement for the purchase and sale of the corner of 14th Street and Indiana Avenue. Subsequently, a 96-unit senior suite building was constructed on the site and has been 100% occupied, with a long waiting list for apartments.

Centennial Court

B.J. Spathies and I decided we would develop the next phase of the townhomes ourselves. I purchased a site at the market rate from the Central Station Partnership. B.J. and I retained MCL to build and sell a development we named

Centennial Court—23 townhomes at the corner of Prairie Avenue and 14th Street. B.J.was designated to head the development of the site and would guarantee the mortgage, while I provided the equity. The Centennial Court units were larger than the previous condominiums and townhomes and proved to be very successful. We were now in an active period in the development of Central Station with the new Prairie Avenue, plus Harbor Club, Park Row and Centennial Court all in various stages of construction.

Prairie Place

Based on its success in the first phases, MCL elected to purchase a parcel of property to be known as Prairie Place. This site was located on the east side of Prairie Avenue and directly opposite the Centennial Court development.

Personal Life Changes
Impact the Development

It was around this time that my wife Georgia and I received news that would change our lives. Georgia was diagnosed with rheumatoid arthritis. Chicago's winter weather seemed to be very hard on her. After careful consideration, we decided to live part-time in Palm Springs, California, where the mild and consistent winter weather and the low humidity of the desert would be helpful in alleviating some of the discomfort she was experiencing.

While Georgia remained at our new home in the desert between late October and early May, I began commuting on a regular basis between California and Chicago. We lived in Chicago the rest of the time, and we moved into Centennial Court to learn more about actual living in that part of the city.

I recognized the need for some changes in our management team and we began interviewing a number of very talented people. I selected Michael Tobin to become president of Central Station Development Corporation. A former architect at Skidmore, Owings & Merrill and a construction vice president for the development of Illinois Center, a large-mixed use project which had also been built over the Illinois Central Railroad, Tobin brought considerable construction knowledge to the Partnership. We were hoping that by having him give our property constant attention, we could move the vari-ous steps in the process faster and better for the future sale of property and construction of improvements.

Relocating Lake Shore Drive

The city, together with the museums and Soldier Field, finally reached agreement regarding the relocation of Lake Shore Drive. However, the city found it did not have sufficient width for the new road at specific points that were adjacent to the Central Station property. A deal was struck in which the Metra Railroad, owner of the tracks, and Central Station, the owner of the air rights above the tracks and some of the fee land, agreed to gift additional property to the city to allow the Lake Shore Drive relocation to take place.

Metra and Central Station negotiated a land swap in which our development deeded a portion of its property to Metra and Metra, in turn, deeded a portion of its property to Central Station. We both then contributed the land to allow Lake Shore Drive to get past the "pinch point" adjacent to Soldier Field. The paper work and negotiations to accomplish all of this took a full year. Mike Tobin handled most of the administration and did an impeccable job.

Acquiring More Properties

While the Metra deal was being negotiated, another interesting situation opened up just south of the Central Station development. The R.R.Donnelley Company, for many years the publisher of the Yellow Pages and a fixture on the city's Near South Side, elected to move from its longtime headquarters on Cermak Road and build a new plant in a suburban location. Donnelley was selling and/or gifting its huge holdings of land and buildings in the area. Although Central Station was offered several of the buildings, we chose to purchase only one property at 1709 South Prairie Avenue, a single story, 133,000 square foot warehouse building with a 44,000 square foot parking lot. We bought this property because it was contiguous to our south 25 acres. Several years later, this site became Prairie District Homes.

—◻—

We decided to purchase other properties to complete our land holdings. I was able to purchase a six-story, 100-unit apartment building at 1221 South Michigan Avenue and a three-story office building with related parking at 1255 South Michigan Avenue. The latter building was occupied primarily by companies in the photographic industry. Both of these properties were adjacent to Central Station's holdings at the corner of Michigan Avenue and Roosevelt Road.

I also purchased a seven-story office building at 1313 South Michigan Avenue, along with two adjacent vacant lots. This building had originally been built for a vertical automobile dealership, but was now a Class C office building.

It was as if all of the sellers thought they had discovered gold. With Central Station as the buyer, the sellers assumed our pockets were deep enough to warrant the extraordinarily high asking prices. Considering that Central Station plans called for tearing down the buildings and using the resulting land, the prices were *extremely* high.

We were convinced, however, the additional purchases were justified in order to complete our land assembly and give us a larger window on all-important Michigan Avenue.

We were able to negotiate what we felt was a fair price for the Donnelley property, though we thought it would not be of significant value for many years to come. This turned out not to be the case. As they say, the best laid plans often take a different turn. With the completion of all these purchases, the partnership had increased its holdings to approximately 80 acres.

Working with Jack Higgins

By 1997, Georgia's rheumatoid arthritis had worsened. Despite the use of state-of-the-art medication to correct and/or slow down the arthritis, her pain, as well as the negative side effects of the medication, had increased. I was concerned I would not be able to maintain my heavy commuting schedule between Chicago and Palm Springs. Albert Ratner and I realized we had come to a point where a decision had to be made as to how to administer the development.

We undertook a major search and interviewed many Chicago developers.

Our choice was the Walsh-Higgins Group. Headed by Jack Higgins, Walsh-Higgins was a diversified real estate development company with experience in all aspects of real estate except residential. Their organization had a strong background in industrial and office buildings, and limited experience in commercial.

Walsh-Higgins was owned by Dan and Matt Walsh, who also own the largest construction company in Chicago (Walsh Construction Company), and Jack Higgins, a former banker who served as the operating head of the company and one-third owner. Walsh-Higgins had been very successful in developing the Blue Cross Building in Chicago and office and industrial properties throughout the country. The firm was well connected within the City of Chicago. We were hopeful they would be able to help in expediting the various stages of the approval process needed to continue developing the property.

Higgins and Central Station had very different views regarding the planning. Once an agreement was reached between us, the architectural firm of Lucien Lagrange & Associates was hired to produce a revised land plan. The street systems were changed and greater emphasis was placed on hotels and offices. The new plan included some of our newer site acquisitions and was showcased with the City Planning Department and the mayor.

The Walsh-Higgins assignment did not include any residential development. That would to be left to me. They hired Jeff Boyle to administer and supervise the development. Jeff had served as Director of Planning for the city and recently returned to the private sector. We cordially ended our relationship with Michael Tobin, who had been president of Central Station, and transferred the files and records from my office to the Walsh-Higgins office.

We had known that Walsh-Higgins owned a large tract of property in the South Loop area, approximately 15 blocks west of Central Station, which could result in competition. Higgins had been in the approval process for that property at the same time he was processing the revised Central Station property on our behalf. Much to the surprise of everyone, even though the parties had been led to believe the city would approve the Higgins plan for Central Station, the only property approval was for this western property. Our process came to an abrupt halt.

We were enormously frustrated, having spent a year replanning the site. We had revised the size of the property and we were stuck without a plan.

The meter was ticking, and we seemed to be getting nowhere with the city. At the same time, much less desirable real estate was being snapped up and converted into all forms of residential properties in the areas all around Central Station. At a time when we really needed something to go in our favor, something did.

Call it coincidence or a twist of fate, but a dramatic medical breakthrough played a critical role in the future of Central Station. A new drug called Enbrel became available to sufferers of rheumatoid arthritis. This life-changing medication enabled my wife Georgia to experience significant and immediate improvement in her arthritis and, in fact, to achieve a reversal of many of its symptoms. The importance of the new drug becoming available to us was not only enormously welcome for our family life, it also

gave me the opportunity to jump back in and take control of the project. I could start commuting again from California to Chicago from late October to early May.

Writing Another New Plan

Albert Ratner and I negotiated the termination of our contract with Walsh-Higgins and returned the responsibility for Central Station to me. With new enthusiasm, I significantly revised the plan, which was presented to the City administration and approved after proper review. It was also agreed that the partners would make a gift of the air rights from 12th Street (Roosevelt Road) to 14th Street to the city with the understanding that, at a date in the future, the city would fund the construction of a platform to hide the railroad tracks from public view and create a park.

Because of the economic recession in the early part of the 1990s, no new office buildings at all were built in Chicago. Additionally, the perception of being so far away from the Northwestern Train Station was a deterrent to office construction at our site. So, by necessity, we had focused on the residential center section, making it considerably bigger. As part of the new plan approved by the city, we created Museum Park, an expansion of the first townhome sections, but this time with both high rise buildings and townhomes. Georgia compared this to an Oreo cookie adding a double filling—we added more cream in the center.

At the end of the day, the result was 75 percent of the total Central Station site area would be residential and, at most, 25 percent would be nonresidential. Central Station was now as I had originally envisioned it, a primarily residential development and, for all the setbacks we had experienced along the way, I was still enthusiastic and optimistic that our vision could become a reality. To do so, however, we had to again restructure.

The Museum Campus and Soldier Field

As the Central Station development was getting fully back on track, the consolidation of the Museum Campus (Adler, Shedd and Field) was being completed. This dramatic new campus captured the attention of both Chicagoans and tourists alike. Nearby, Miegs Field, a quasi-private airport, was scheduled to un-

dergo a conversion of its own and would revert to being known as Northerly Island. The property would become a park adjacent to the Museum Campus in the year in 2002 or 2003. The Museum Campus, made possible by the reconfiguration of Lake Shore Drive, was a major asset to Central Station as its most proximate neighbor. More than five million people visit the three museums each year with that number steadily increasing.

Years before it became nationally known as the site of the Chicago Bears' home games, Soldier Field was an important part of Chicago's landscape and history. In the 1909 Plan of Chicago, Soldier Field is noted as the city's "athletic grounds" and was regarded as monumental even then. It was constructed at a cost of $6 million, its classic columns of reinforced concrete—much of it pre-cast in the form of cut stone—built to last through the ages. It has been compared to the Parthenon or the Coliseum of Rome. Dedicated to the memory of Chicago's men who sacrificed their lives in war, historians have written that it symbolizes in its classic architecture, in its beauty and its strength, the youth and courage and the will to win—the spirit of the city's young manhood of 1917.

That Soldier Field is virtually steps away from Central Station creates yet another link to the history and the greatness of the city. In 2001, the city and the Chicago Bears' owners reached an agreement that called for the renovation of Soldier Field. The project, which began in 2002, is expected to take two years.

Museum Place

To capitalize on Central Station's location next to the Museum Campus, I entered into a contract with Robin Development for the construction of two high-rise condominium towers, to be called Museum Place. The development was to be situated on the property we had purchased at 1304 South Indiana Avenue. Central Station agreed to "contribute" our land into a joint venture to be matched by money from the Robin Group. The two companies would jointly develop the two condominium towers. This was the first of my "new strategic joint ventures." Solomon Cordwell Buenz & Associates were chosen as architects and two 23-story condominium buildings were designed to be constructed on a phased basis.

Several years before, we discovered that under a portion of the 1304 site was a pumping station built in the 1800s and covered with about 20 feet of earth. Robin expressed serious concerns about the bearing capacity over this buried building for their first tower.

STS, a well-known consulting firm, was brought in to perform extensive tests on the property. Although these tests indicated the proposed building could be supported, Richard Robin was still deeply concerned. Despite his feelings, he agreed to open a sales and marketing center and we achieved a good level of sales for the first building, to be known as Museum Place I. Capitalizing on its proximity and the "borrowed" value of the nearby Museum Campus, Museum Place sold 70 units within the first few months.

Part of the development was the construction and dedication of a park at 14th Street and Indiana Avenue. This park was to be built by Central Station and presented as a gift to the City of Chicago. In September, 2000, construction was completed and the Daniel Webster Park was deeded to the city.

A 44,000 square-foot park at the corner of 14th Street and Indiana Boulevard, the park was designed to provide a relaxing ambiance to the area. Its entrance is graced by four large pergolas welcoming visitors to the park. The park is directly opposite the 1304 site and the first proposed tower.

Even with this initial sales success, the Robin Group and I were divided in terms of our respective philosophies. Robin had concerns about the pumping station. Although units continued to sell, he was backing away from the deal. Albert and I worried that if this high visibility development were to be abandoned, it would have a significant negative impact on the entire Central Station project.

We had succeeded in rezoning the property, and the Chicago housing market was beginning to take off. I had revised the development plan, taking it back to the original concept of primarily residential units consisting of high-rise, mid-rise and low-rise. We desperately needed to come up with a solution for the imminent Museum Place problem.

We had been looking for the right organization to develop the other residential properties that were now zoned between 13th Street and 14th Street. After interviewing a number of well known Chicago developers, we entered into an agreement with The Enterprise Companies, the family-owned company of Ronald Shipka Sr. and his two sons, Ronald Jr. and John. The contract and joint venture agreement was for the property east of Museum Place, to be developed with both low-rise and high-rise residential units.

Museum Park

It was clearly just a matter of time until Robin would want to be released from his contract. In anticipation of that, we created an alternative plan in which Central Station and the Shipkas would develop what was to become known as *Museum Park*, only in different phases than had been previously outlined.

In June 1999, Robin asked to withdraw from the transaction and assign all of the plans, contracts, obligations and liabilities to Fogelson Properties in return for a full release.

Working around the clock with Shipka, we quickly changed plans utilizing the land that had been intended by Robin for high-rise buildings to townhomes and transferred the high-rise density to the opposite side of the street for new high-rises and townhomes.

Museum Park would now be an 860-unit condominium development consisting of three 20-story buildings, townhomes and a private recreational and health club. It would be the largest condominium development in downtown Chicago.

We continued to work with the architects on planning, and we made a rather bold decision to offer the units for sale before we had any actual models that prospective buyers could walk through.

(Above) Grant
Park/Museum
Campus
pedestrian
access at Lake
Shore Drive

(Left) Museum
Campus-Shedd
Aquarium &
Field Museum

(Left) Centennial Court: 23 Townhomes, Fitzgerald Associates Architects

(Below) View looking south from Museum Park Tower 1 at Webster Park, Centennial Court and Prairie Place

(Above) Prairie Place: 96 Townhomes,
DeStefano + Partners

(Left) Park Row: 68 Townhomes, Fitzgerald
Associates Architects

(Above) Harbor Square:
80 units, Roy H. Kruse
& Assocs. Inc.

(Right) Senior Suites,
Mann Gin, Dubin &
Frazier, Ltd.

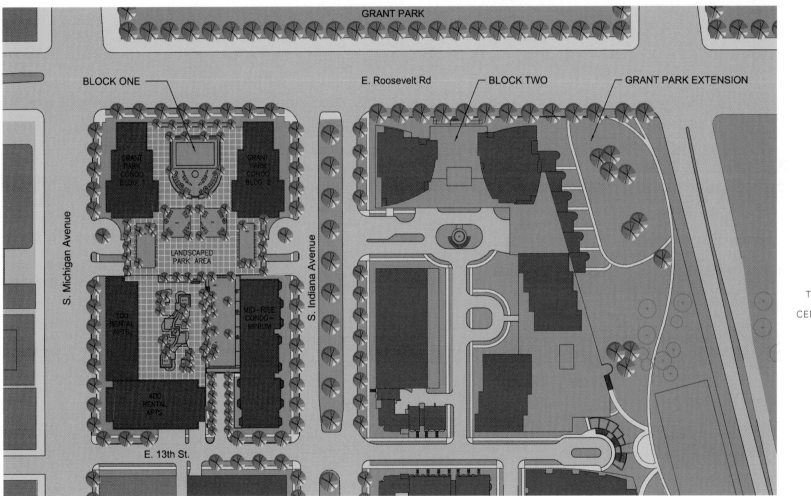

GRANT PARK

BLOCK ONE   E. Roosevelt Rd   BLOCK TWO   GRANT PARK EXTENSION

S. Michigan Avenue

GRANT PARK CONDO BLDG 1

GRANT PARK CONDO BLDG 2

LANDSCAPED PARK AREA

S. Indiana Avenue

100 RENTAL APTS

MID-RISE CONDO-MINIUM

400 RENTAL APTS

E. 13th St.

Enlarged Block 1 site plan

(Left) Rendering of proposed Indiana Avenue streetscape with mid-rise condominiums in Lakeside on the Park

(Below) Rendering of proposed Roosevelt Road streetscape looking east from Michigan Avenue and Roosevelt Road

(Above) Rendering
of proposed
Michigan Avenue
rental apartment
building at street level

(Right) Rendering of
proposed roof deck
above the parking
garages on block 1

Museum Park
Community Center,
Pappageorge/
Haymes, Ltd.

Museum Park-Park
East Townhomes:
36 Townhomes,
Pappageorge/
Haymes, Ltd.

Night shot looking north from Museum Park Tower 1

Aerial view of Central Station, Museum Campus, and Soldier Field

Aerial view of Grant Park from Central Station

(Above left) Construction view: 15th & Prairie

(Above) Prairie House: 187 units, 6 Townhouses
DeStefano + Partners

(Left) Prairie Tower: 162 units, DeStefano + Partners

(Above) Prairie District Homes, Phase 1 &1A:
49 Townhomes. Warman, Olsen & Warman, Ltd.

(Right) Prairie District Homes:
177 units, Warman, Olsen & Warman, Ltd.

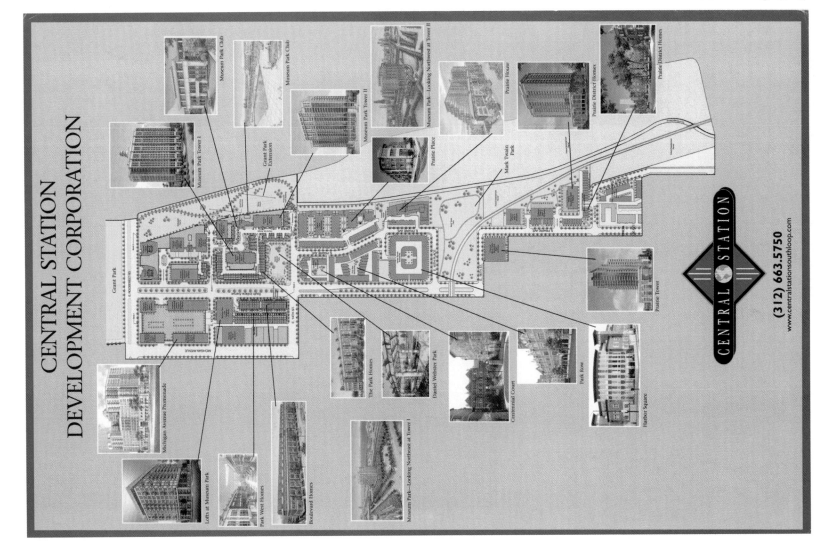

CENTRAL STATION
DEVELOPMENT CORPORATION

CENTRAL STATION

(312) 663.5750
www.centralstationsouthloop.com

Museum Park Club

Museum Park Club

Museum Park Tower I

Grant Park
Extension

Museum Park Tower II

Prairie Place

Museum Park—Looking Northwest at Tower II

Prairie House

Prairie District Homes

Prairie District Homes

Mark Twain
Park

Grant Park

Michigan Avenue Promenade

Prairie Tower

Park Row

Harbor Square

Lofts at Museum Park

Park West Homes

Boulevard Homes

The Park Homes

Daniel Webster Park

Centennial Court

Museum Park—Looking Northeast at Tower I

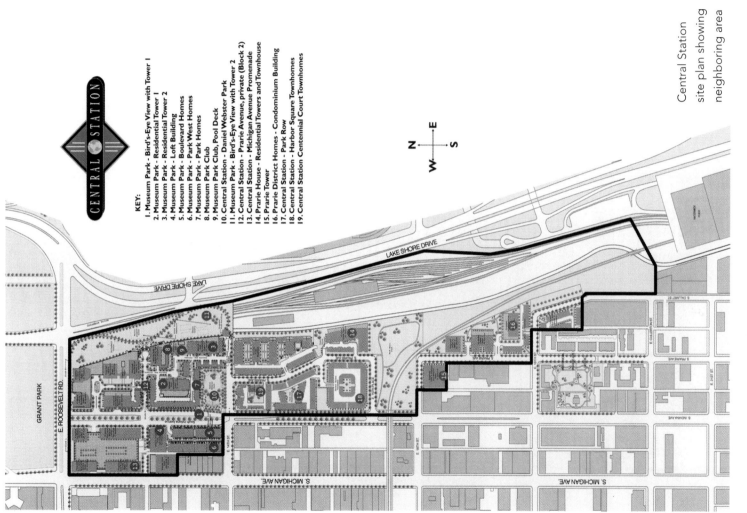

SITE PLAN

KEY:

1. Museum Park - Bird's-Eye View with Tower I
2. Museum Park - Residential Tower I
3. Museum Park - Residential Tower 2
4. Museum Park - Loft Building
5. Museum Park - Boulevard Homes
6. Museum Park - Park West Homes
7. Museum Park - Park Homes
8. Museum Park Club
9. Museum Park Club, Pool Deck
10. Central Station - Daniel Webster Park
11. Museum Park - Bird's-Eye View with Tower 2
12. Central Station - Prarie Avenue, private (Block 2)
13. Central Station - Michigan Avenue Promenade
14. Prarie House - Residential Towers and Townhouse
15. Prarie Tower
16. Prarie District Homes - Condominium Building
17. Central Station - Park Row
18. Central Station - Harbor Square Townhomes
19. Central Station Centennial Court Townhomes

Central Station
site plan showing
neighboring area

(Left) Museum Park Tower 1: 221 units,
Pappageorge/Haymes, Ltd.

(Above) Museum Park Lofts: 149 units,
Pappageorge/Haymes, Ltd.

(Right) Museum Park Tower 2: 170 units,
Pappageorge/Haymes, Ltd.

(Left) Museum Park Tower 2 and
Soldier Field as of July 2002

(Above) Indiana Avenue
lanscaped and lighted median

(Above right) State-of-the-art
Central Station development
office and model

(Right) Daniel Webster Park—
one acre, Daniel Weibach &
Partners, Ltd.

(Left) Firehouse Restaurant
(Above left) McCormick Place—"McCormick Square" main entrance
(Above) St. Charles Railroad Trestle over Indiana Avenue

A sales center was created on the east side of Indiana Avenue, using specialized trailers, again designed and leased by Riha Design. With scale models, floor plans, elaborate brochures and artists' drawings, this very engaging and attractive facility offered a *vision* of what the development would ultimately be.

We retained FireStar Communications, a marketing firm run by Ron Cohn and Harvey Haddon. Their considerable creative talent, as well as their extensive experience in Chicago real estate, made them a good choice to take on the marketing of the development. They created superb ads and brochures that emphasized both quality lakefront living and the unique history of the area.

People who had purchased units at Museum Place were contacted and were asked to come in, one by one, for private presentations and a look at the new plans for Museum Park. They were then offered a choice of either having their money returned immediately or selecting a townhome or condominium at Museum Park at a significant discount to compensate for any inconvenience the delays may have caused them. Special deals were structured that would allow them to transfer their contracts from the Museum Place development on the west side of Indiana Avenue, to a unit of their choice on either the west or east side in Museum Park. An astounding 92 percent of the buyers decided to stay in Central Station

and purchase at Museum Park. Those who chose not to take advantage of this offer simply cancelled their contracts, satisfied that they had been treated well.

Enterprise Companies had recommended the architectural firm of Pappageorge/Haymes, Ltd. for Museum Park. George Pappageorge, a designer, and David Haymes, a pragmatic architect, head a 25-person firm that specializes in condominium and residential developments in Chicago. Pappageorge/Haymes had completed several projects for the Shipkas, and Shipka insisted that the firm's top man, David Haymes, and crew chief Jeff Renterghem be assigned to the development.

We decided to reduce the density previously approved on the west side of Indiana Avenue and develop that site with four-story townhomes. Brick, renaissance stone and copper accents were chosen for the exteriors. A total of 36 townhomes, ranging in size from 2,017 square feet to 2,807 square feet, and with one- and two-car garages, sold-out quickly. In addition, we offered 23 larger townhomes with two and three bedrooms and three to three and a half baths. These townhomes sold very rapidly, confirming our belief that the market was ready for a higher-priced quality unit and that concerns about the development's location were no longer the obstacle they had once been.

The east side of Indiana Avenue would be developed

in three phases. We designed upscale townhomes to be built around Daniel Webster Park. Thirty-six of these Park Homes, ranging in size from 2,395 square feet to 3,332 square feet, all with two-car garages and a minimum of three baths, sold immediately.

The first high-rise tower was to offer 19 floors of living space above three floors of parking with units ranging in size from 804 square feet to 1,339 square feet. The building was to be a painted concrete design, with balconies and brick and renaissance stone at grade level. Many extraordinary features, such as a deluxe lobby, an entertainment room, and other amenities were designed into the product.

Museum Park Tower 1 was very well received. We sold 70 percent of the units (169 sales) within five months of the opening, and we were 95 percent sold-out by July of 2001.

Our plans for the east side of Indiana Avenue also called for the construction of a major clubhouse and pool facility to be located in the center of the development, with a concierge service, business center, party room, recreational facilities, and an outdoor pool and sundeck that overlooked the Museum Campus and Lake Shore Drive.

The Museum Park Club would cost nearly $3 million and would be for the exclusive use of the owners and residents of Museum Park. No other Chicago condominium development had ever planned or built so extensive a recreational facility.

The second phase of Museum Park, Tower 2, would consist of 170 units that would range in size from 1,300 square feet to 2,076 square feet. Construction of the building was scheduled to start in August of 2001, to be followed by Museum Park Tower 3 and the remaining townhomes. Tower 2 has larger units than Tower 1 and a richer amenity package. An amazing 65 percent of the units were sold before we broke ground.

The total Museum Park plan, therefore, would consist of a total of 860 units of condominiums and townhomes. It is an ambitious plan, and we believed we made excellent use of the land and the views, at the same time, bringing to the public what it wanted. The look and quality of the development seemed right for the times, yet suggested images as elegant and tasteful as their names implied.

A Key Addition to the Central Station Team

Albert Ratner hired Jerry Ferstman, an attorney who had previously worked with Forest City, to be the liaison between Forest City and our Chicago office. With the departure of Mike Tobin, who had been president of the development, Ferstman was given the responsibility of finding the right person for this key position. We created a job description that highlighted the qualities we were looking for. When Ferstman saw Tim Desmond's resume, he immediately called me.

I knew instantly that Tim was the right man for the job and set out to convince him to join us. After meeting with me on several occasions, he flew to Cleveland to meet with Albert, who agreed with our choice. Tim Desmond was named President and Chief Operating Officer of the Central Station Development Corporation. A graduate of The University of Detroit with a degree in architecture, Tim had begun his career with the prestigious firm of Skidmore, Owings and Merrill. Through several years there and after leaving, he acquired tremendous knowledge and experience. This included working with Richard Stein, one of Chicago's more prominent and successful developers, on the expansion of McCormick Place—an experience that made him familiar with the Central Station area.

Tim immersed himself in the history of the development, meeting with key members of our team and establishing an excellent rapport with each of them. We set our goals and objectives for the year and then divided them into quarters and, later, into specific months. We budgeted monies needed to reach these new goals, and we evolved a working arrangement wherein I made the major deals with builders and others and then worked with Tim and his staff on implementing the terms of these transactions. We touched base with each other every day in order to review the important items on our agenda—both large and small—and assure no time was wasted.

With Tim on board and our ability to work well together, we were able to move quickly in addressing our agenda. Many individual items required longer amounts of time. In real estate, the most time-consuming items are the legal matters and areas that involve working with government. The numerous contracts, leases, agreements, title issues, loan documents and joint venture considerations take enormous amounts of time. Lawyers are especially concerned with details and operate with extreme care.

We had the most complicated planned unit development in the history of Chicago real estate, and, as such, each phase required extensive review and interaction, first with the Planning Department, then with various agencies and departments of govenment, such as transportation, underground utilities and others. When that was done, there was still the matter of securing building permits, occupancy permits, and on it would go.

It is fair to say that Central Station was and still is the most scrutinized real estate development in Chicago. It is also the city's most visible development, with thousands of cars passing it each day on Lake Shore Drive, Indiana Avenue and Michigan Avenue, in addition to the millions of people who visit the area to visit the Museum Campus and the millions more who attend the high profile events at McCormick Place and Soldier Field.

Because of the size and scope of the project, we reduced it to sections, with each section having its own list of what needed to be done and the amount of time allocated to do it. Tim recruited his own staff and developed a computer program system that enabled him to juggle many aspects of the project simultaneously and still keep it all moving forward. Every time he thought he was catching up, I would make another land purchase or create another joint venture for him to add to his list. We worked together in the most harmonious and, I think, effective way since that day we exchanged promises to each let the other do what we do best.

Prairie House

When B.J. Spathies left The Fogelson Companies, she took on a number of projects, both on her own and with other developers. I was well aware of her considerable abilities and subsequently sold a section of Central Station property to her. This site in the middle of the property is where B.J.'s BEJCO Development Corporation is building Prairie House, a 14-story, 183-unit high-rise condominium building at the northeast corner of 15th Street and Prairie Avenue. With DeStefano + Partners as the architect, the building's one- to three-bedroom apartments range from 800 to 3,000 square feet. A unique feature of the building's design is the stepped terraces facing north from the 4th through 14th floor.

Before any construction on Prairie House could begin, however, it was necessary for B.J. to go through numerous community development meetings because the Prairie House site was now surrounded by the homes we had originally developed at Central Station—Harbor Square and Park Row—and those neighbors had the opportunity to learn what was being planned. The alderman in the ward is Alderman Burton Natarus, one of the city's truly pro-development elected officials. He supported B.J.'s plan. Prairie House is a very successful development with units scheduled to be delivered in 2002.

Prairie Tower

One day, early in 2000, Tim Desmond and I climbed up onto the St. Charles' tracks, which are elevated about 20 feet at that point. Central Station owned a small piece of property at the southwest corner of 16th Street and Prairie Avenue, just south of the St. Charles Airline. From this perspective, we saw for the first time that there was a small building adjacent to the property we owned. It had been used for many years as a place to store transported automobiles. If we could buy that building, tear it down and combine the land with what we already owned, we would have a great site.

Early in 2001, we took title to that property. We subsequently tore down the building as planned and entered into a contract with B.J. Spathies to put up another condominium building, to be called Prairie Tower. Seeing the building and putting the property together with our own site was not really the trick. The smart move was realizing that the parking for a new condo building would have to come up out of the ground in order to provide enough parking spaces for the building's occupants. Therefore, the first "living" level—that is, the actual apartments in the building—would start 40 feet in the air, and every other "living" level of Prairie Towers would have fabulous views of the city and the lakefront.

Instead of the railroad being an impediment to us, it presented an opportunity.

When we presented this idea to B.J. and her architect, DeStefano + Partners, they got it immediately. We had previously built Mark Twain Park across the street. Therefore, every unit in this beautiful building would overlook the park and have panoramic views looking north or northwest or east or southeast. The design of the building takes full advantage of the site.

We had created a fabulous site by putting the pieces of land together.

Prairie District Homes

The Legacy Development Group, a company we had been favorably impressed with, was developing a building near Central Station. Legacy was started by Warren Barr and Bill Warman. Barr had been an executive with a large suburban builder, The James Companies. Warman is an architect who, with his father and brother, own an architectural practice in Chicago.

I had been contacted by Garry Benson, who had been with MCL when our two companies had been involved in a joint venture development in Antioch. After he'd gone on to form his own marketing and sales group, Garrison Partners, and had considerable success with various builders in the city, including Legacy Development Group. Garry told me they were working on several deals and suggested we meet with Legacy.

Tim Desmond and I met with Warren Barr and Bill Warman and took an immediate liking to both men. They had put together a good organization and were eager to work with us, particularly in the vicinity of 18th Street, where we were looking to create a new relationship.

In most respects, the deal we structured with Legacy was similar to the arrangement we'd struck with Enterprise Companies for Museum Park. Warren Barr would vote on decisions on behalf of Legacy and I would vote for Forest City/Fogelson. The transaction with Legacy Development Group was handled by Tim Hildner, who had previously worked for Illinois Center. Legacy's sales and marketing team included Garry Benson's Garrison Partners, and Deborah Johnson and her daughter Emily of Taylor Johnson Associates, who would handle advertising, public relations and the production of marketing material. Riha would again create the sales center trailer. Richard Levy of Schain, Burney, Ross and Citroen provided Central Station's legal representation, as the firm had for several years.

In all, 49 townhomes and 180 condominiums were planned for the first phase.

After considerable discussion, we decided to call the development Prairie District Homes. This would enable us to borrow the prestige associated with the Prairie District and identify the location. Our theme would be built on the fact that this location was long associated as the site of the best homes in Chicago and, with this development, would regain that distinction once again.

The Prairie District series is as significant a component of Central Station on the south as Museum Park is on the north. Prairie District Homes is also important because it is located in a part of Chicago that has such a great story with the designated Historic District, the new developments by Rezmar and other real estate developers, and the recent creation of Hillary Rodham Clinton Park.

It should be noted that the north and south sides of the development are not meant to directly compete with one another. There are several differences between Prairie District Homes and Museum Park. For example: both the townhomes and condos in each development are different—Prairie District Homes condos are somewhat smaller and the buildings are brick. Museum Park's units are larger, higher-priced units constructed of concrete.

Prairie District Homes overlook Burnham Harbor, while Museum Park units look north and east.

Prairie District Homes was planned for townhomes and two condominium towers to be built on a former parking lot and the site of a torn-down single-story building. When completed, this will be a $600 million to $700 million project. The townhomes opened in the last week of July of 2001 and sold 35 of 49 units in less than three weeks. The surrounding area has undergone a "gentrification" and the best properties in that area are in Central Station, largely because of its spectacular location close to the lake.

The condominiums opened in September 2001, one week after terrorists' attacks on America created a worldwide state of shock. Still, 25 percent of the building sold within a week, an indication of both a resilient public and an appreciation of what we had to offer.

St. Charles Airline

The St. Charles Airline, which, despite its name, had bifurcated the city of Chicago for many years, cutting through it like a knife since the beginning of the 20th century. It was originally designed to serve the R.R. Donnelley plant and was later used by many railroads, including Amtrak, as a turnaround point. While the needs of industry may have been well met a century ago, the St. Charles Airline at the start of the 21st century was largely a structural and aesthetic barrier to the economic, social and cultural renewal of the South Side of Chicago. The city has been trying to get rid of it since 1920, especially more recently, since Donnelley left the area. This "removal" has been a high priority of the city and virtually every planning group for years.

In a report prepared by the City of Chicago for presentation to the federal government, it was noted that "Areas including Chinatown, Dearborn Park, the Prairie Avenue Historic District and Central Station are profoundly impacted by a largely obsolete transportation impediment. The St. Charles Airline also perpetuates the physical and psychological separation of these neighborhoods from the Loop and the Lakefront, and limits visitor access to the area."

The St. Charles Airline is owned by several railroads, including the Canadian National, Illinois Central, Norfolk Southern, and Burlington Northern-Santa Fe. All of the railroads agreed finally, after decades of discussion, to relocate the St. Charles Airline. It was determined that if such a relocation were to occur, the benefits to the city in general—and to our community in particular—would be phenomenal. The Weldon Yards would be moved; the many overpasses cutting through the South Loop could be removed; hundreds of millions of dollars of development land would be opened up; and the tracks running along Lake Shore Drive could be concealed from view.

Environmental benefits of such a relocation would include reduced noise pollution along lakefront parks, the elimination of diesel pollution along the south lakefront, elimination of risks from hazardous materials moved by freight trains running below the nation's largest convention center, and reduced or eliminated risks from soil contaminants typically associated with railroad operations.

Metra would benefit from improved operating efficiencies, minimizing freight travel times and reducing track maintenance costs, among other considerations. Both Amtrak and the various freight lines would realize significant benefits as well. McCormick Place could expand to the north, the public could enjoy greater ease of access to Lake Shore Drive and to Soldier Field; and a development could be created on Central Station property to take full advantage of the available fiber optics. An opportunity would exist for creating an east-west transportation connection at 16th Street or 20th Street, similar to what Central Station was able to create at Roosevelt Road.

To Central Station itself, the importance of the reloca-

tion of the St. Charles Airline is immeasurable because we own all the air rights above the St. Charles and above the Metra tracks for that entire 25-acre area of the city.

Albert Ratner and I met with Mayor Daley to urge the adoption of a creative relocation plan. We suggested that no one had looked at the whole picture or had considered the obstructed views, noise pollution and development opportunities. Past efforts had never really explored the enormous benefits that could accrue to all sides if a relocation could be arranged.

The City administration agreed immediately and requested we meet with the commissioner of the municipal Department of Transportation to help formulate a proposal for the relocation.

The people who built Central Station continue to help change the tone of a city, one note at a time. The final decision for relocation has not yet been made.

13th and Indiana

The Central Station team had originally targeted the corner of 13th Street and Indiana Avenue for a high-rise building to be used for assisted and independent senior housing. In 1999, Senior Lifestyle's chairman, Bill Kaplan and I entered into a contract to develop a 20-story senior housing structure on this site, subject to certain contingencies. In the middle of the year 2000, the environment for senior housing changed substantially. Most public companies involved in that sector saw their stocks plummet, and the availability of financing dried up. The contract for this property was therefore terminated.

At this point, I again studied the situation and determined another use for this property would be as a midrise rather than a high-rise. The property was adjacent to our upscale townhomes (Museum Park West). In looking at the entire program, the Central Station partners realized they could have a more compatible use.

The Shipka family agreed that a new "loft building" would be an appropriate design for this site. A contract was entered into for a development to be known as Museum Park Lofts, which would be a joint venture between the same parties that had developed Museum Park (Fogelson, Forest City and the Shipkas).

Pappageorge/Haymes was again selected as the architect, and a building was designed to be 15 stories high over three levels of parking. This building would be unique in the category: it would have the benefits of being a "new loft" with all new systems, and still preserve the features that had proved to be so popular in the loft market in Chicago, such as high ceilings (to 10 feet) and large balconies. Loft-type floor plan units were designed. The new building would also carry the Museum Park Lofts name, which the partners believed had significant value because of the early success of the Museum Park development.

In July of 2001, we opened for sales, having built a model at the sales and marketing center. The first one-third of the building sold quickly, and construction started in June of 2002 with more than 100 of the 149 units sold.

The 1300 Block of Michigan Avenue

As a result of this decision, property that previously had been acquired at 1313, 1319 and 1321 South Michigan Avenue was reevaluated by our team. I had purchased the property to protect the rest of our site from structures that might have a negative effect.

In 2001, a plan was evolved to tear down the 1313 building and to acquire a building to the immediate north—1305–1307 South Michigan, a two-story property occupied by a labor union.

We designed a new building that would extend 176 feet north and south on Michigan Avenue by 130 feet deep.

The building would have two floors of retail shops and businesses, which were needed in the area, and the second phase of the Museum Park Lofts located above. This plan made good business sense to me. The loft program, designed on the 13th Street and Indiana Avenue site, could be continued. Lessons learned from the marketing of the first building could be incorporated into the marketing and design of the Michigan Avenue Phase II loft building.

A further benefit of this development would be the ability to provide up to 20,000-plus square feet of space for retail establishments and service businesses, such as dry cleaners, Starbucks Coffee, Kinko's Print Shop, a restaurant, and the like. As this book goes to press, we have not yet determined when this site would break ground.

McCormick Place, Our Neighbor to the South

McCormick Place, Chicago's imposing convention center overlooking Lake Michigan, first opened its doors in 1960. The first building was located on the east side of Lake Shore Drive. From the start, that location stirred debate because of the Lakefront Protection Ordinance and the strong feelings held by many preservationists and others that no commercial buildings should be situated on the lakefront. In the end, economics won out, and the city's most modern convention center was built and became a great success.

In 1967, the building was destroyed by fire and had to be completely rebuilt. The East Building was constructed on the original McCormick Place site and reopened in 1971. Its architect was the noted Helmut Jahn. Despite the fact that the rebuilt structure was larger than the original building, demand for space soon exceeded capacity, and a second structure, the North Building, was built on the west side of Lake Shore Drive in 1986. Yet another structure, the South Building, was added providing the facility with nearly 3 million square feet of additional convention space. A new, larger hotel was built as well. Now, with some 6 million square feet of space, McCormick Place is the largest convention center in the United States. Expansion plans have been approved and yet another phase of McCormick Place will begin in 2003.

The Busway

The entire City of Chicago experienced a period of substantial growth between 1993 and 2000, and the city's traffic congestion increased along with it. To alleviate traffic, a Busway connecting McCormick Place on the south with Chicago's hotel district on the north was designed. The Busway cuts travel time and stress for area residents and visitors to the city. It will reduce the time it takes to get from Soldier Field to the Millennium Park parking structure. The nation's largest convention center was especially affected. The busway became operational in 2002.

Technology

Any discussion of "life in the city of the future" inevitably turns to technology. Most of the major fiber optic lines that serve the Chicago metropolitan area converged immediately south of the city, since most of the fiber optic lines run along the rights-of-way of the railroads and/or under the tunnel system that serviced Chicago. At the beginning of the 21st century, this is a very important consideration.

While Central Station purchased the former Donnelley property at 1709 South Prairie, the main Donnelley building, known as Lakeside Press, a 1 million square foot historic building, was acquired by a development group from New England, which planned to convert it to retail space and rental apartments. That same group also purchased the adjoining Donnelley buildings, which were not landmarked. Where once developers, as well as much of the public, seemed to dismiss the area—regarding it as a less than desirable place to build or live—the tide had clearly turned in a very major way.

In 1998, the Lakeside Press building was sold to The Carlyle Group and Co-Relocation Group from Washington, D.C., for the purpose of creating a "carrier hotel" that would provide facilities for all types of electronic transmission for a variety of telecom companies. The building is perfectly suited to this purpose because of its heavy floor load capacity, the presence of centralized heating and chilling from the McCormick Place construction and substantial electric power capabilities needed for this type of facility to operate efficiently, dependably and successfully. It fit well in the city of the future. History seemed to have come full circle, but history has a way of playing tricks. With the demise of so many dot-com companies and the bankruptcy filing of huge, once-powerful companies such as Global Crossing, this building found itself in financial trouble in mid-2002.

Grant Park Towers

On Block 2 of the development, Grant Park Towers will offer what many people believe is the very best location at Central Station and perhaps the best location in Chicago. The preliminary plans by Pappageorge/Haymes show buildings with unobstructed views straight north over the park and harbor. Such a view has never been experienced in Chicago because the area has never before been developed. No specific start time has been established.

Chicago's South Loop: Since Central Station

To many people, Central Station will always have a strong identification with the Illinois Central railroad and Chicago's history. But consider what today's Central Station has done to make its own mark and create benefits for both the community and the city:

- Lake Shore Drive, Roosevelt Road, Indiana Avenue, the parks and the Museum Campus are some of the important touchpoints that owe their major improvements to the creation of Central Station.
- Better access to roadways, improved transportation and view corridors to Lake Michigan are among the changes that have defined the community.
- New homes and enhancements to the area have brought a richness, style and elegance to the community.
- Central Station donated the land that became the south end of Grant Park, and by making a gift to the city of air rights, the tracks from Roosevelt Road to 14th Street will be covered for improved aesthetics and a more inviting access route to enjoy the park.
- The area just west of Central Station has developed into a growing stretch of retail shopping outlets with new Dominick's, Jewel/Osco, and Walgreen's stores.
- The area continues to evolve and thrive with the construction on Wabash and State Streets and new academic facilities along Michigan Avenue.
- New construction and renovation have characterized the area, bringing major improvements and a proliferation of restaurants, galleries, stores and shops; plus the further expansion of Columbia College and other institutions that would likely not have been undertaken without Central Station as the driving force of the community.

We played a small role as well in making possible the expansion of Soldier Field, the city's premier outdoor stadium, and in completing Grant Park. Soldier Field was built in 1927 at a cost of some $6 million. In the summer of 2001, the Illinois state legislature approved a plan to rebuild Soldier Field at a cost of nearly *$600 million*. The construction of a proposed deck over the railroad tracks from 12th Street to 14th Street, with a park that will offer both active and passive attractions for the general public, will greatly enhance the area.

The proximity of world-renowned educational institutions—the University of Chicago, University of Illinois, Roosevelt University, Columbia College and others—and the city's world-class museums and galleries and Orchestra Hall, home to the Chicago Symphony, reflect the intellectual, cultural and aesthetic sensibilities of the area. Access to the business and financial district, shopping, fine dining and *fun* dining, entertainment and perhaps the best mass transit system in the United States, is further proof that the "central" in Central Station is an appropriate designation for its quality of location and quality of life.

Museum Park—with its Residential Towers, Lofts, Boulevard Homes, Park Homes, Park West Homes and the Museum Park Club—along with Park Row, Mark Twain Park, Daniel Webster Park, Harbor Square Townhomes, Centennial Court Townhomes, Grant Park Towers, Prairie District Homes, Prairie House with its Residential Towers and Townhomes, and Prairie Place:

These and many other buildings planned but not yet named are some of the reasons why Central Station, richly reflective of the history of Chicago, is truly "the city of the future." After years of relative inactivity—even abandonment—the area is alive again.

Past, Present and What's Ahead for Central Station

The first days of 2001 were much like those of the year before. There were some "warning signs" of what was to come. The hysteria over the "dot-coms", the technology industry and the exhuberance in the economy in general had started to diminish. The economy seemed less buoyant, and although business was still quite good, the overall atmosphere had turned more guarded.

Economists and the business press were predicting the U.S. economy would remain strong. The market was simply experiencing "a negative blip," they said. Meanwhile the housing market—particularly in the city of Chicago—was beginning to show signs of a slowdown.

In early 2001, the stock market, which had risen to risen to dizzying heights, fell precipitously. Federal Reserve chairman Alan Greenspan moved swiftly to cut interest rates. These short-term rates did not register much of an impact on the long-term rates; however, developers and builders whose construction financing was tied to an index saw the cost of their construction loans drop. Buyers were able to secure lower-cost mortgages, due to the interest rate drop.

By the summer of 2001, the sales of new homes at Central Station had slowed, while some other builders in Chicago were not selling at all. In Chicago's suburbs, the situation was quite different. Lower interest rates—and the ability to fix mortgage rates—and an enormous amount of refinancing activity led to near-record sales.

In the city, the housing market was not good and builders were eagerly anticipating the fall selling season. From September to mid-November is traditionally a good selling period in the housing industry. But the events of September 11, 2001—events that permanently changed the lives of so many people in the United States and around the world—determined this would not be a traditional season in any respect.

The attacks by terrorists on U.S. sites created an uncertainty that would linger for years. Most activities of all types came to a halt. Decisions were postponed. Bankers, builders and everyone else waited to see what long-term impact these events might have on our way of life.

In the real estate market, most sales centers' levels of activity slowed dramatically and, predictably, so did sales. However, Prairie District Townhomes' sales center, which had opened September 18, 2001, experienced an amazingly positive response, selling 25 of 49 units in its first two weeks. The initial sales of the Prairie District Tower condominium that opened in early October of 2001 were similarly strong. While sales were off from previous years, Central Station was doing better than other developers and builders in the city.

Central Station had initiated a "branding" effort in the second quarter of 2001—a program aimed at creating a neighborhood identity. Mounting an aggressive public relations campaign and a massive program that included newspaper ads and direct mail, Central Station invested a substantial amount of money to bring its story to the community. This campaign differed from the type of advertising the builders were doing and was directed and financed by Central Station. While each of the builders promoted their own line of housing and products, Central Station was promoting the area and the neighborhood it was creating.

And the effort paid off. Further, people began to see Cental Station as Chicago's next Lincoln Park. This image was reinforced by the high-rise buildings of Museum Park and Prairie House, visible from all directions on Lake Shore Drive and Michigan Avenue. The noticeably heavy activity in townhomes and other construction in the area further reinforced the sense of energy in the community.

By this time, Central Station had more to offer than ever before. Legacy Development Group was selling Prairie District Townhomes and the Prairie District Tower; BEJCO had Prairie House and its new development, Prairie Tower; Enterprise was marketing Museum Park Tower 2 and the Museum Park Lofts, in addition to completing the sales of units in Tower 1. Construction activity was heavy, with as many as 700 people working on various buildings throughout Central Station. Therefore we were much more of a presence in the community.

Interest rates continued to fall (the Fed had lowered interest rates at least 12 times between the first quarter of 2001and the third quarter of 2002.)

September 11, 2001 had changed everything, and its effects will be with us for years to come, but by December of 2001, sales at Central Station were again on the rise. In fact, in a month that is typically weak for home sales, December 2001 sales exceeded sales of the previous December. We regarded that as a positive sign. Albert Ratner and I believed the United States and its people were capable of dealing with anything that came their way. We began moving forward, secure in our belief in our country and its resilience.

Central Station was outselling the competition. We credited that to its location, high credibility and the variety of products we had brought to the market. We could now fix dates and deliver. We were getting referrals. Our efforts at branding, along with the builders' ad campaigns, were showing results. The media was taking notice of Central Station and coverage of what had been developed—and what continued to emerge—was overwhelmingly favorable.

Central Station had become known as a real estate development offering quality products and good value at fabulous location.

Albert and I decided the time was right to begin the final planning and development of Block 1, the 3.92-acre super-block bounded by Roosevelt Road on the north, Michigan Avenue on the west, Indiana Avenue on the east, and 14th Street on the south.

Working with Ronald Ratner, head of the Forest City Residential Group, we developed a plan that called for nearly 500 rental apartments. The first rental units at Central Station, these would consist of approximately 100 units designated as affordable senior units and 400 of our most luxurious one-, and two-bedroom units, including 20 percent affordable.

In preparing our ambitious apartment plan, we called upon John McCormick, who was the head of tax incremental financing (TIF) for the city. The Central Station TIF we had created in 1991, which had been expanded to become the Near South TIF, is and will be the most successful tax incremental financing effort in the history of the state of Illinois and the city of Chicago. By 2014, when that TIF expires, it is projected to accumulate more than $700 million of surplus money for the city—*after* having paid-off the the bonds and having covered the cost of a new school on Cermak Road. Beyond 2014, the taxes generated by this TIF will be even greater, once the responsibility for the bond debt is removed. From an economic perspective, Central Station is proving to be one of the all-time great catalysts, providing major benefits to the city.

In January 2002, we outlined our rental apartment plans to the Department of Housing and the city Department of Finance, as bond financing would be required. Both agencies expressed interest in the proposed plan, so we retained Solomon, Cordwell and Buenz to design the first rental complex at Central Station. We also reached agreement with Legacy Development Group for approximately 160 condominium units at the southesat corner of Block 1—the intersection of Indiana Avenue and 13th Street and planned to start marketing in October of 2002.

The resulting plan for Block 1 is shown on page 58. It includes two Grant Park condominium buildings that will overlook Grant Park at the corner of Roosevelt Road and Michigan Avenue, and Roosevelt Road and Indiana Avenue, as well as retail space on Michigan; an apartment complex at the corner of Michigan and 13th Street; and another condominium at the corner of 13th Street and Indiana.

Encouraged by the success of Prairie District Townhomes and Prairie District Homes, we also decided to complete the planning for the south end of Central Station. This was important since we hoped to finalize the relocation of the St. Charles Airline in the near future.

Once the plans for the south side of the property are completed, the city could make its determination as to the additional amount of tax dollars and economic activity that could be generated, as well as determining the what funds would be available to help in the relocation of the St. Charles, and other city projects.

The planning for all of Central Station was essentially complete, subject to the usual modifications that changing times and circumstances demand.

By May of 2002, 100 of the 145 loft units were sold prior to groundbreaking. Museum Park Tower 2 had sold more than 120 of its 170 units by May 1. People began moving into Tower 1 and sales throughout the Museum Park project continued at a healthy pace. Museum Park

Tower 3 is planned and scheduled to begin offering units for sale in the fall of 2002.

On a related note, the Chicago School of Real Estate at Roosevelt University, the school I envisioned and helped to make possible, in 2002 had achieved a $3.5 million endowment and announced that John DeVries would become the Director of the school and would also occupy the Gerald W. Fogelson Chair in Real Estate. This marked the first time any university in Illinois had an endowed chair for the study and teaching of real estate.

The years it has taken to create Central Station seem to have flown by. As I look over the development now—and the community it has become—I think of it as all my friend and mentor Leonard Schanfield imagined it could be and more!

When will the plan for Central Station be fully realized? That question is difficult to answer. As this is written, sales at Central Station continue at a vigorous pace and construction goes on. The area that has been so significant a part of Chicago's history and has become, to most people in the city, an exciting emerging neighborhood; but to a very select group of people, it is *home*.

In Their Own Words:
The People Who Built Central Station

Albert B. Ratner

Albert B. Ratner is chairman of Forest City Enterprises, a publicly held diversified national real estate company that develops, acquires, owns and manages commercial, residential, hotel and retail properties throughout 21 states and operates regional offices in New York, Los Angeles, Boston, Tucson, Washington D.C., San Francisco, Chicago and its headquarters in Cleveland. Among Forest City's signature properties are MetroTech in Brooklyn, New York; Fairmont Plaza in San Jose, California; Securities Industry Automation Corporation (SIAC) in New York; Millennium Pharmaceuticals, a joint venture with MIT in Boston; the redevelopment of Denver's former Stapleton Airport; Millender Center in Detroit; NYMEX in New York; and Chase Manhattan Bank in New York City. Forest City was also selected as the developer for the 1.1 million square-foot Kings County Family Court and New York Supreme Court Criminal Court project in Brooklyn; and for the New York Times $175 million dollar headquarters in New York City.

"My relationship with Central Station started when I was in New York City at our office, trying to decide whether or not we would buy something called the Barton Candy Building. It was an old candy factory in Brooklyn, and we had concluded that it might be what we needed to provide some space for government offices. I was really concentrating on this and had asked not to be disturbed, which is something I don't do very often.

"But I was told I had a phone call from my wife's attorney, Leonard Schanfield, who said he had a client with a piece of land on Lake Shore Drive. He started to describe the property and said he really thought I should take a look at it. As I was focused on something else, I asked him to just tell me how much money we were talking about. He told me the price. I closed my mind and thought 'there's some disconnect here. I'm thinking about a building, and he's talking about a property for a similar price. Something didn't sound right. He promised to get back to me with more information.

"About ten minutes later, I received another telephone call from my wife's accountant, Paul Anglin, who gave me about the same speech I had just heard from Leonard Schanfield. I was interested enough that I made arrangements to fly to Chicago, meet Jerry Fogelson and take a look at this piece of land.

"What I realized in looking at the land—and what Jerry confirmed—was that in Chicago, everything was laid out in such a way that everything had streets running through it, but this piece of land did not have streets running through it, which I thought was advantagous, because, it was always my belief that Chicago had great buildings, but not great projects. That is to say, that the individual buildings were fantastic and there was great architecture, but when you have blocks that are intersecting without knowing what's going to go there, it's tougher to create great projects. We can talk about a series of wonderful Chicago buildings, but there's not the symmetry that comes from using a great amount of open land to create a project. I thought this was a real chance to do something.

"I thought the land would be great for creating back-office space for corporations, as I was doing in Brooklyn. I thought I could do exactly what I was doing there and transpose it to Chicago. It was logical to me and made a lot of sense. What I discovered, however, much to my chagrin, was that in Chicago, for some reason, corpora-

tions at that point were not doing things the same way as New York corporations.

"Jerry Fogelson had said all along that the property should be residential. We were both right in that we couldn't put in buildings for commercial use because people hadn't accepted the location for commercial use—even though I still think it is a phenomenal commercial location with parks, museums and a great quality of life. In New York, if we put a half-acre park in the middle of Brooklyn, it's as if we created ten Rockefeller Centers. But if we had developed at that time strictly for residential use, there wasn't a market for it. The property was an enigma. In the minds of people in the area, it was so far away, yet it was in reality so close physically.

"Jerry and I visited Mayor Rich Daley, who had been newly elected. We started talking about the South Side of Chicago, knowing of course that the mayor was a South-Sider and he shared his view with us, that the next great growth in the city of Chicago would come from the south side. That was important for me to hear. We made plans, put in streets, built some residential units and began to offer them for sale. It's fair to say that when Mayor Daley himself bought a home here, it certainly gave us impetus.

"Part of our business is trying to project what things are going to be like in the future. What's happened to us in most of the places we've built is that the success we've had has been as much because of what other people have done. We started here, and we established this clearly as a good neighborhood. This opened the door. Loft buildings were converted into condominiums.

"We found ourselves in the middle of a real South Side revolution in which people who are buying homes here that never imagined they would buy homes on the South Side. People from the North Side and the suburbs have been attracted to this area.

"Looking back, the decision that this is a great piece of real estate was clearly right. The idea that the South Side would gain in acceptance was clearly right. What was wrong, on my part, was how the property would end up being used. I thought it would be more of a mixed-use development, where it has become largely residential. But when you look at the history of Chicago, along Lake Shore Drive and around the park system, it's basically residential. My view now is that it makes sense.

"One way you judge a development is by how well people have done who have purchased homes there. I think the people who took the initial gamble on Central Station have had excellent returns. The reason is the view, the proximity to the city and the assets, such as being able to walk to the museums or a Chicago Bears football game, are overwhelming.

"What Mayor Daley has done to beautify the city is unique in all the world. He seems to have changed expectations and convinced people that it's possible to live in a great city that really **is** a great city. A good deal of the credit has to go to the mayor for how his outlook has affected what we have been able to do at Central Station.

"At the end of the day, when people look back on this project, they will see this is one of the great residential projects ever done in this country. I would like to say that is because of Jerry Fogelson's brilliance and my brilliance, but the truth is that it is because there is the lake and parks. The view from Central Station, looking out at the city of Chicago, Grant Park, the lake and the museums is a unique view anywhere in the world. We didn't create the lake, Grant Park and the museums. All we can take credit for are the buildings. We've become the first beneficiaries of location, location, location. But the ultimate beneficiaries are the people who live here — they and their children are the beneficiaries. It's a unique place with a great story. I am proud to have been able to work with Jerry in creating this development."

B. Timothy Desmond

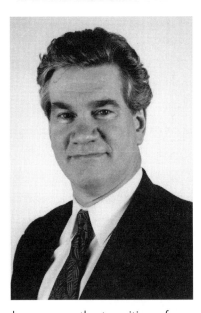

B. Timothy Desmond is the President and Chief Operating Officer of the Central Station Development Corporation. A licensed architect with more than 26 years experience, he is recognized for his significant management, design and construction expertise, particularly in developing major projects. He was the development executive on the $400 million Town of Fort Sheridan redevelopment project, where he oversaw the transition of an army base to an upscale residential community. As the general manager of development for Mc3D, the develop/design/build team assembled by Stein & Company for Chicago's $675 million, 2.9 million-square-foot McCormick Place South Building expansion and 800-room Hyatt Hotel, Mr. Desmond was responsible for development issues, including zoning, entitlements, code and management of design/build teams. His extensive experience includes having been a Managing Director of the respected firm of Mesirow Stein Real Estate as well as working for leading development and architectural firms, including Skidmore, Owings & Merrill, The Linpro Company, and Perkins & Will Architects.

"At the time I became president of the Central Development Corporation, the plans called for condos, town homes, commercial and retail components, perhaps the most expansive and versatile undertaking in the history of Chicago real estate and certainly one of the most interesting and challenging developments of my career.

"Central Station attracts a diverse group of home buyers—museum buffs, lakefront joggers, cyclists, Grant Park music festival fans or just anyone who enjoys being at the center of the urban scene. But they are diverse in other ways as well. People who relocated to the suburbs and, with their children now grown up and out on their own, don't need the big houses anymore, wanted an excellent 'quality of life' community that represents the best of what Chicago has to offer.

"The spectacular views of the lake—actually the best of any point in the city—and access to parks and the museums in a secure and historic property, have attracted many of these people, who had planned to move back into the city some day. But it's not only the so-called 'empty nesters', it is their children, young professionals who may work downtown and want to be near their jobs or just prefer living in the city. Central Station offers an interesting mix of the energy and vibrance of the city and a beautifully constructed community.

"The master plan envisioned a mixed-use development with high-rise office, condominium or rental buildings along the perimeter of the site and low-rise development centered on Indiana Boulevard. By planning the site in this way, existing neighborhood ambiance is enhanced and maintained, and provides an excellent view of the surrounding amenities. Additional plans included seniors' residences and rental properties.

'This is a historic area, but it is much more than that. Central Station has brought stability and prosperity to the entire neighborhood. It has become the most active growth area in Chicago. The infrastructure within this neighborhood is unlike any other system in the Chicago Central Business District. Broad tree-lined boulevards enhance the area and serve as extensions of Grant Park, connecting Central Station to the center of the city. Roosevelt Road and Indiana Avenue each has landscaped median strips and parkways along the entire length of the street. Carefully planned design guidelines have protected the views of the lake and the park for all neighbors within Central Station. We are extremely proud of what we have been able to create. My relationship with Jerry Fogelson has been fabulous. He is the CEO and Chairman and I am the COO and President. We have meshed well and have been able to accomplish our goals and objectives without sacrificing our principles and high standards. And we are having fun.

"As the new century began, we counted some 50 new developments underway in the area. Just a decade earlier, no one would have dreamed that would be the case. The fact that Central Station achieves harmony with the park and the lake and serves as an enduring extension of the vital downtown and lakefront area has made the city one of the most exciting and livable cities in the United States."

B.J. Spathies

B.J. Spathies, the Founder and CEO of BEJCO Development. Formerly the president and a junior partner in the Fogelson Companies, she began BEJCO in 1993 and is recognized as a highly successful land acquisition specialist. She assembled the land for The Oak Club, a luxury townhome development at Oak and LaSalle Streets, the former site of Henrotin Hospital. Among her most notable successes are The Residences, a prime riverfront location opposite historic Wolf Point on the western edge of Chicago's River North neighborhood;

The Residences of Sauganash on the city's Far Northwest Side; Chatham Club in the Chatham/Chesterfield area on the Far South Side; and The Residences of RiverBend, a 37-story riverfront high-rise in Chicago's Fulton River District. While with the Fogelson organization, she helped to assemble and develop 1,000 acres of land in Northern Lake County (Wadsworth and Antioch, Illinois). Ms. Spathies is the developer of Prairie House, the mid-rise development consisting of 184 condominiums and four townhomes on 15th Street in the Central Station development.

——◻——

"I spent a very long time working with Jerry Fogelson, coming up through the ranks or, as he calls it, the 'Horatio Alger-ette Story'. I remember when we acquired the IC property. Jerry found the piece of land and, to his credit, it was one of the best kept secrets in town even after it was acquired. It was the piece of land everyone drove passed, but never really noticed. Its only real distinction was people remembering it was where they parked and crossed over the bridge to go to the Bears game. It was a true find. Jerry happened to get together with IC Industries at the time they were prepared to divest themselves of some assets, and this turned out to be one of those really great assets.

"One of my mentors—and one of Jerry's as well—was Leonard Schanfield from Rosenthal and Schanfield. He thought a good partner for the Fogelson Companies would be Forest City and he sort of married the two entities together. My primary role was to handle a lot of the documentation. I did the loan agreement, went to the closing and subsequently worked with the city on the TIF, the tax increment financing. I basically handled the detail work that Jerry hates to do. I was intimately involved in that part of the transaction, acquiring and getting the TIF through the city and handling all the documents that went with that, which was a laborious process. It was a bit of a coup to get that kind of a TIF on this project. It was something that was absolutely needed, but nevertheless sometimes government agencies don't see the need. We have to give them a lot of credit for seeing it in this case. I think it's made a huge difference in the South Loop area.

"When you drive through Central Station now, you really feel you've entered a place that is its own little enclave. As soon as you drive out, you know you've left Central Station. There is something about the streets and the architecture and the way that it's done that is very special unto itself.

"We had divided the site into three distinct increments at the beginning. We really felt that the northern-most section should be offices and some kind of facility, the central portion would be residential and the southern portion, with air rights, should be more institutional, vis a vis a hotel to serve McCormick Place, etc.

"Unfortunately, even with the best divisions, the market doesn't necessarily go with that. It was never intended from the beginning that as much residential property would go into the site as subsequently has. But that's been the train driving this engine. And, frankly, I think the residential component brought greater value to the site than if the partners had waited, hoping for that big building or back-office user or whatever they were hoping would come in on the North Side. I think that what's gone in there has been higher-end, architecturally pleasing and the way the plan has been laid out really lent itself to this. . . .

"There absolutely was a vision. Was that vision realized? Not yet. Is it going to be what was envisioned back in '89? No. But it's better. As time evolves and you see what's needed, I think it is going to actually turn out better than what was anticipated.

"My own building, Prairie House, looks at Soldier Field. The Museum Campus, the park and all the amenities all the way to the lake are incredible. To me, there is no better view in the city of Chicago than driving north from McCormick Place up Lake Shore Drive. You get it all—the lake, the museums, the high-rises, it's just a breathtaking view and Central Station is now a very big

part of it. It used to be the old expression 'you can't get there from here,' but now you can. It's all in one place . . . bridged together. I was pleased by how many people want to live there. It's hard to compare it to anything.

"No doubt about it though: Jerry is the driving force that has made all of this happen. If Leonard Schanfield were still alive, I know he would be proud of what is being accomplished."

John J. George

John J. (Jack) George is a partner in the law firm of Daley and George, specializing in general corporate legal matters, commercial litigation and real estate law. A former Assistant Attorney General and former Assistant Corporation Counsel for the City of Chicago, he has argued cases before the Illinois Appellate Courts and the Illinois Supreme Court, as well as before Federal Appeals

Courts. Mr. George's numerous public and community service projects include the Little City Foundation, where he has been an active Board member and general counsel since 1976; his active participation as a member of the Civic Advisory Board of Hinsdale Hospital; and his service on numerous committees of the Chicago and Illinois Bar Associations. He is actively involved in the work of numerous charitable organizations, including Xavier University, St. Ignatius College Prep, Catholic Lawyers Guild and Old St. Patrick's Church.

—◻—

I think the first time Jerry Fogelson and I met was in 1989. He called me and I met with him in his office where he discussed with me his vision for Central Station. Jerry had a tremendous enthusiasm for the project. In my way, I always listen and don't comment on what I'm thinking until I've had a chance to assess something in its entirety. So at that first meeting, I listened and I was not as enthusiastic as he was. He saw this and asked me, 'Aren't you enthusiastic?' And when I said that I was, he added 'It's a monster of a project.' I said it's going to require a lot of hard work and should be great if it really happens.

"At that time, Jerry was represented by Rosenthal and Schanfield, who were the lawyers for the land acquisition. Leonard Schanfield, I recall, was a highly respected lawyer and a truly fine man. I was asked to work on the plan development for the project. Because of the size of the project, which really would be the biggest real estate development of its kind in the United States, and it would take a lot of hard work to bring it to conclusion They had at that time a very different vision for Central Station than what it ultimately became. The original proposal called for a lot of tall, high-rise buildings—office buildings and a big office complex that would take over much of the entire site. They had a lot of ideas about big corporations coming there, big companies taking some back-office space and things like that. So when we did the master plan and the guidelines, that's how we did it. We went off on that approach, expecting that was how it was going to be developed.

"As years passed, during the early 1990s when the real estate market went through some really bad times, that vision wasn't able to come to fruition. The big office users, the big 'box' users, were just not investing or going forward with those kinds of projects. So they had to reassess where they were going. What they did was decide that from at least 14th Street south, they would develop the propery for residential use. They came up with the concept of Central Station with townhomes, apartments and condominiums.

"The one thing that should be noted is that Central Station, it's been my belief, has been responsible for bringing back the South Side of Chicago, certainly the Near South Side of Chicago. Had it not been for Central Station, I don't think the South Side would have developed the way it has and I think that goes in large measure to the credit of Jerry and Albert. There were, at that time, few developers in the nation that had the staying power that those two men had, that allowed them to hold onto that property and go forward with the development—not that other developers wouldn't want to have gone forward and done what they did. But these two men just could do it because of their expertise and their backgrounds and their financial ability. Others would not have had that. But they stayed and they developed it and it really started to take shape and to draw the attention of a lot of people.

"First, the type of product they put up was really a very, very nice product. They also developed Indiana Avenue and created a boulevard from Roosevelt Road south which really created a great entrance to Central Station. They also worked extremely hard with the Department of Planning and other city agencies to create a new Roo-

sevelt Road from Michigan all the way over to the Outer Drive, which now is really a beautiful roadway, not only from a traffic standpoint, but from an architectural standpoint as well with the way the bridge has been done.

"What was accomplished here really was a great accomplishment of course by Fogelson and Ratner, but also to a large extent by and with the city of Chicago. At that time Jeff Boyle was the planning commissioner. He was a man with a good deal of vision, who worked very hard to put into place both his own vision as well as that of the mayor of the city of Chicago, Mayor Daley. The mayor was always very enthusiastic about having this whole area developed because he believed that it was an area that would attract a lot of people. So from the time that they brought the concept to him up until today, he continued to feel very strongly about the Near South Side of Chicago being developed.

"Over the years, the property has been developed with beautiful housing and it was all done pursuant to our master plan and our guidelines. We had to revise them of course because our master plan initially had a different vision for what was going to happen over there. We always had to go back in and get permission to accommodate the changes. I think this particular development, Central Station, was put under more scrutiny than almost any other planned development in the history of Chicago at that time.

"Because it was not just one parcel, but many parcels that were going to be developed in phases over time, the city required that we have a master plan for the various blocks and how they were going to be created. Then we were required to create design guidelines, open-space guidelines, all sorts of guidelines that we would integrate as part of these development phases as they occured. Those guidelines were approved by the city council, approved by the plan commission, and each step along the way were developed with the insight and review process of the city with respect to facades of the buildings, elevations, landscaping and such details being developed in that fashion.

"As Central Station was being developed and people saw what was happening there, other developers began to undertake developments outside of our Central Station complex, all along Michigan Avenue, Indiana Avenue, farther south, State Street. . . . Go up and down those streets now, from the river east to the railroad tracks and from Roosevelt Road to 22nd Street, and you will see developments there that no one ever thought would occur. Buildings that were eyesores have been converted into beautiful loft buildings and condominium buildings and the whole area has taken on a neighborhood atmosphere.

"Commercial development has occured down there and on Roosevelt Road with huge supermarkets and all sorts of other commercial developments coming in to support all the residential users that have come in. Each one of the buildings put in was the subject of a review process by the planning department—all the input in all aspects of the development.

"We tried to develop along Michigan Avenue, in addition to residential properties, some newer planned buildings for educational uses and professional offices, all to enhance the whole neighborhood. Other buildings are incorporating retail businesses on the first floor, providing needed amenities such as drug stores, cleaners and coffee shops so that people living there now can walk out their front doors, down blocks and enjoy the neighborhood experience in their own community.

"Our role as the land-use attorneys is to assist clients who are developing properties that must be developed under what we call a plan development process. The whole idea of a plan development as opposed to a rezoning of property is that in a plan development, when a plan development is approved, it has much stricter controls that become part of the ordinance and that differs totally from a rezoning. When a property is rezoned, for example, from an R4 to an R5, then anything that's permitted in an R5 can be done. But in a plan development, you have what is called a bulk table that becomes part of the ordinance and sets forth the FAR—the floor area ratio—which tells you how big a building you can put on the property, any setbacks, elevations, materials that will be used on the building and types of landscaping that will be done. All these things become part of the ordinance, so that when a plan development is approved, a developer cannot deviate from what he proposed to build to what he is actually going to build.

"It is a great comfort to a community to have a plan development put in place because the community is included in meetings and its input is incorporated into the plan before going to a plan commission hearing. We did that in this case. We incorporated input from the community into what we did.

"People are moving back to Chicago in great numbers because I think they have a great comfort in what Chicago's about now. They realize that the museum campus that was created in this area is not just for Central Station, but for everyone. We have some of the best museums in the world and people in Chicago really enjoy them. And the lakefront is the most beautiful lakefront in the world. You can travel anywhere and nothing matches Chicago. People can see that. The Convention and Tourism Bureau has sent out questionnaires and is getting back responses from people all over the world who have travelled here and have given their impressions of Chicago. People are saying Chicago is a beautiful place. Our schools have gotten so much better and so has our transportation system. There are a lot of things that are driving people back here, younger people who want a first-time place are coming in and making a commitment to stay. People who may have lived in suburban areas and are growing older and their children have either gone away to college or have gotten married and they are finding that they're moving back because they want to take advantage of all the cultural events and want to be in close proximity to them, not have to travel for an hour to get here.

"All along the lakefront, things are booming because people really believe in Chicago, in the administration of the city and in Mayor Daley. They like the way he manages the city and what is happening here. They have a strong hope that it's going to continue. . . . We agree with them."

Ronald B. Shipka

Ron Shipka, Sr., is head of The Enterprise Companies, a Chicago organization with more than three decades of experience and a reputation for innovative design, quality construction and for undertaking "impact projects" that distinguish them as one of the most versatile and successful real estate developers in the Midwest. The firm's portfolio of developments includes new construction as well as rehabilitation projects—from townhomes, single family homes and loft developments to commercial and mixed-use projects. Recognized for its expertise in creating vibrant residential communities from dormant urban sites, Enterprise's developments have made a visible impact on the neighborhoods in which they are located. Projects such as Landmark Village and the Lincoln/Belmont/Ashland redevelopment have received national recognition for their ingenuity and creativity. Enterprise has consistently been rated among the 400 largest residential development companies in the United States and has developed more than $500 million in real estate in recent years. The Enterprise Companies' successful projects in the Chicago area include Henderson Square, Altgeld Commons, Terra Cotta Village, Carriage House Lofts, Seminary Commons, Ravenswood Park, and The Regal Lofts. Museum Park is The Enterprise Companies' elegant and dramatic project at Central Station.

—◻—

"Museum Park is an integral part of the overall Central Station property. The project started with relationships that Jerry Fogelson developed over about 10 years with various developers who created the first approximately 240 townhomes. Jerry came to us years before with a presentation that left us amazed. We were in his offices on Dearborn Street and had gone downstairs to the presentation room. Here were my son John and I viewing a presentation where Jerry was talking about moving Lake Shore Drive and about this huge piece of property. . . . We couldn't believe that anybody could actually pull this thing together and get it going. But he did.

"So, fast forward to ten years later. Jerry sat down with Ron Jr., my older son, and John and myself and we made a deal. It's been a huge success.

"Phase I of the Museum Park project consisted of 36 back-to-back townhomes at one site, 23 townhomes at a second site, and a series of additional townhomes located at a third point, around the park, and the first Tower building. It has been a terrific success with all these townhomes sold in a relatively short period of time and now under construction. The Tower building was 85 percent sold in an amazingly short time.

"We opened Tower 2, and it was 55 percent sold almost immediately. We went forward with building a loft building, which would be a different style of building that would appeal to a more entry-level and first-time home buyer, not only in the style of the building, but in the finishes that are inside it. That is Phase 1, Phase 2 and the Lofts. We are now working on Phase 3. Of the projects we've done of a similar magnitude, Museum Park has been by far the most successful insofar as sales are concerned and initial construction. It has worked out very well.

"An important part of the project is The Museum Park Club, the community center located next to Tower 2. It is a $3 million facility and the center of our concierge services for all of Museum Park. It has a party room, pool table, fully-equipped kitchen, locker rooms and an outdoor swimming pool and a sun deck. This is expected to always be exclusively for the residents of Museum Park.

"In addition, we created a Loft building with a whole series of upbeat features. The facade is recessed behind a grating system of metal with vines growing around it, rather than a simple type of balcony arrangement. Inside are 10-foot ceilings. It is a very interesting building.

"In order to enhance sales, we built models of typical units in Tower 1 and Tower 2, the Loft Building, and furnished them, all at the sales center. People were able to see pretty much what they were getting. In the selection center, our sales associates and design coordinators sit down with the homeowners and select the hardwood flooring, carpeting, kitchen cabinets, all of the faucets and vanities and trims.

"Museum Park is a place of sophisticated homes that set the standard for city living. It is a community where people can live stylishly, elegantly and have all the treasures of the city just steps away. No other part of Chicago offers the proximity to the city's best recreational and cultural facilities. And it is part of the Central Station neighborhood which has achieved premier status in downtown living."

David A. Haymes and Jeff A. Renterghem

David Haymes is a Principal and Jeff Renterghem an Associate with the architectural firm Pappageorge/Haymes Ltd. The firm is noted for its respect for the history of the urban environment. Based in Chicago, Pappageorge/Haymes played a major role in the development of Museum Park and lists University Village, Old Town Square, Orchard Park, West Market Place, and the Kenwood/Oakland Master Plan among its most significant projects.

"We first met Jerry Fogelson when he was looking for an architect and had put together a kind of mini-competition. Jerry had become friends with a client of ours and as a result, we were asked to participate. That was how we were introduced to the Central Station project.

"At the time it was a major investment on our part because we were not inclined to work for free. But we were enticed nonetheless because of our relationship with Dan McLean of MCL Companies. Ultimately we were not successful in the competition, coming in as the proverbial second-place choice. But we have to say that over all these years, Jerry has not changed at all in terms of his energy for this project. He is amazingly focused.

"Somewhere along the way Jerry asked us to become involved working directly for Central Station, doing feasability analyses for various parcels of land, studying a wide range of ways it could be used, and mostly focusing on the eastern portion of the site. We were studying older co-op style approaches, but that never went anywhere.

"Our present relationship with Central Station came about through our relationship with The Enterprise Companies with whom we'd worked at that point for some 10 years. Jerry was considering options for partnering, chose Enterprise and that's how we became involved. We had just come off another project with Enterprise—Kinzie Park, a very large scale multi-product type of development, and a co-project of Enterprise and Habitat. It was very successful and similar in spirit in that it was a mixture of tall buildings and smaller, neighborhood-size townhomes. And the nature of the relationship was similar in that working with co-developers we had been essentially serving two masters. An interesting dynamic happens when you try to develop tall buildings and short buildings all at the same time and how those things relate to each other. It is necessary, too, to understand that all of the participants have certain expectations—the city had expectations, the developers had expectations, certainly we had expectations.

"We sort of knew that we were a part of something very big, but we were focused on only a relatively small part of the whole Central Station project initially. We learned about the scope of Central Station in general, but since our focus was a specific project, we didn't absorb as much as we might have.

"We knew from day one that whatever we would do on the part of the property called Block 4, which is a piece of property that will have unobstructed views from now until the end of time—we knew what we were stepping into. We had a really strong sense of the importance it would have—and there was a great deal of excitement about that and how that was going to effect the northern skyline of Chicago and how we were going to have a chance to complete the South Side. We called it 'the postcard' because we knew that whatever was going to be built here was eventually going to be a part of the postcard that would change the city's skyline. Once we figured that out, we really felt like big shots. But it drew our attention to just how big what we were involved in would be.

"We never knew we would become so involved in the project. Our role has evolved to much more than we thought it would be. We never envisioned by year 2000 we would be building these high-rises and see it all come alive so quickly.

"The architecture itself is an important part of this. The two residential blocks that had been completed when we started had a very historical, traditional character. Museum Park was to take that direction. They didn't have to push us too hard as we saw it that way as well. As we progressed, our interests evolved. Enterprise and Fogelson and we had a great interest in seeing residential housing being produced.

"What is a new, exciting loft space supposed to be like? Inside, we focused on creating a staid appearance, more in the historical direction. A major step was to learn to 'speak loft'. Selling the concept was not easy. It was a major event for us to prevail in terms of the direction the building could take.

"We applaud Jerry for having an open mind. He started with a very specific direction that Central Station would be very traditional, but allowed it to evolve to include a lot of ideas. They have allowed us to be architects and we have been able to feed off their ideas as developers.

"Museum Park, because of size and type, is still about how buildings relate to one another. We were allowed to let buildings play off each other.

"With regard to Grant Park Tower I, they couldn't say enough: a crisp, modern building. For us, that's pretty juicy stuff—one hopes to be able to get into stuff like that. We are building view corridors that will be the best in the city. That's pretty spectacular. As we're moving north, we are pulling back layers of history—underground tunnels from 100 years ago. We are challenged by such an infrastructure.

"We have a sensitivity to the way Michigan Avenue and, generally the neighborhood, have been built. Central Station made us, as a firm, step up to the plate in how we do business. The development team recognized the value of each individual building. This was about differentiating. It's not one building over and over—every building is about how it relates to the others, but each is very differ-

ent. We fought the very 'suburban idea' of the same building over and over.

Burton F. Natarus

Burton Natarus is the Alderman for Chicago's 42nd Ward. He was first elected in 1971 and, as this book goes to press, he is serving his eighth consecutive four year term representing the 42nd Ward in the City Council of Chicago. Alderman Natarus is a member of the Mayor's Zoning Reform Committee and the Central Area Planning Task Force. He is the former Chairman of the Committee on Landmarks Preservation and has served on numerous key committees and task forces, including the Housing and Real Estate, and Zoning Committees and the City Task Force on Land Use, the Lake Michigan Shoreline Subcommittee, and the Chicago Plan Commission. A practicing attorney in Chicago for more than thirty years, Alderman

Natarus is the recipient of many prestigious awards. His strong support of the development of Central Station over the years proved invaluable.

—◻—

"Central Station is important to Chicago. I know Jerry Fogelson has been working on it for a long time. He deserves a tremendous amount of credit, not only for his insight and his foresight, but for his perseverance. He was determined that Central Station would succeed.

"I think it was Rosenthal and Schanfield who convinced him to take on the project. But Central Station sparked development in an area that was never thought of as a site for a mixed-use community. There were businesses there and certainly Donnelley was a major presence in the area, but no one saw what he saw.

" Jerry's brilliance here was in the fact that he saw the residential potential of that property before anyone else. He had the insight to see that people would be moving back into the city in significant numbers. He recognized that the area was changing, but he didn't only meet the change, he sparked the change.

"All of the buildings have contributed something. He hired good architects and that can be seen—the innova-tive integrating of high rise buildings surrounded by townhomes is an excellent system, unlike most others.

"While people are moving back into Chicago all over the city, Central Station is unique and has a great deal to offer in terms of its location and its architecture. A development like this attracts a variety of people. Some of the early buyers were short-sighted and were trying to keep new people out of the community. The reason that's short-sighted is that a community needs numbers of people moving in before the government can help. We see numbers and that guides us in planning and funding and building schools and libraries—the things that help provide a sense of community.

"The density that concerned some of the early residents creates traffic, but that density and traffic is what attracts retail businesses and other commercial establishments that all add something to the community.

"Central Station was a catalyst, responsible for rehabbing a high school in the area and for a new school being built as well. A teacher's academy is also being built near there. The main police station is there. The city can take responsibility for such matters as handling the traffic, but what the development has done in its buildings and in attracting people and business to the area is something the city could not do.

Daniel E. McLean

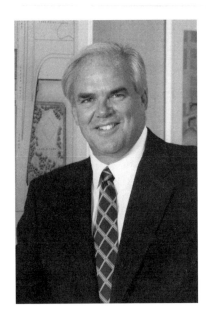

Dan McLean is President and Chief Executive Officer of MCL Companies. Created in 1976, the company specializes in the development, construction and marketing of urban properties. Before that he was a banker for five years. He was the first president of the Chicago Home Builders Association. MCL is a national company with offices in New York, Miami, Chicago and Denver. Among the firm's standout projects are Prairie Place at Central Station, The Embassy Club, Cornell Square, RiverView Condominiums at River East, The Pointe at Lincoln Park and Altgeld Club.

"Jerry Fogelson's group approached us because we were building Dearborn Park 2. Jerry was taking the plunge with Central Station. They offered us one parcel and asked what we could do with it.

"We brought in five architectural firms and asked them to give us proposals. We expanded the original plot to two plots—two different parcels—to create Harbor Square and Park Row. Originally the site was going to be only Harbor Square, but they liked the scheme so much, they said to do two at the same time. One was going to be a little bit less expensive. Then we built Centennial Court for Jerry and B.J. That was the third part. Prairie Place came next.

"There's been a huge demographic change of people living in the city. The market in the eighties was probably 500 units a year, and now it's grown to be 3,000 units a year in downtown Chicago. We certainly see the change. The market was more of the baby boomer generation deciding that they didn't want to live in suburbia—or if they did, it was only for a few years. Then they came back to downtown. The city kept the original, younger population and added empty nester-baby boomers that wanted all the things that the city offers.

"Chicago has some wonderful things going for it. The fact that it's so diverse, economically and industry-wise, has helped it to withstand the huge economic downturns. Chicago is certainly one of the most stable cities in the United States, if not the most stable. It doesn't see the booms and the busts.

"If you want to buy a house that appreciates five percent every year and you'll always be able to sell it, in good times or bad, that's one of Chicago's strengths."

The Architects

In telling the story of Central Station and the people who built it, credit must be given to the nine major architectural firms that played such an important part in making Chicago's largest real estate development a reality. This extraordinary wealth of talent represents a developer's Dream Team:

DeStefano and Partners, a large architectural firm in Chicago, is headed by Jim DeStefano who became recognized internationally when, as the Managing Partner of Skidmore, Owings & Merrill, he achieved considerable success in London, England. DeStefano + Partners has done a great deal of planning work for Central Station in connection with the master plan and served as the architects of Prairie Place, Prairie House and Prairie Tower. The firm has also acted as planners for Central Station's south 25 acres and as such has played a key role in the development as both planners and architects.

Lucien Lagrange and Associates is a highly creative and internationally respected architectural firm. Among the firm's best known projects are the Park Hyatt Tower Hotel on Michigan Avenue and renovation of the historic Insurance Exchange Building. The firm was retained by Central Station and worked closely with the organization as the land planners responsible for revising the north end of the property, as well as the revised PUD plan.

Roy H. Kruse & Associates, Ltd. served as architects on Harbor Square. Over more than 30 years in the profession, Mr. Kruse has appeared to offer his expertise before the Chicago Planning Commission, various Zoning Boards of Appeals, building departments, and both the Department of Housing and Urban Development and the Illinois Housing Development Authority. Before starting his own general architectural firm in 1973, he was associated with some of the leading architectural firms in the profession—Mies van der Rohe, Robert Babbin and Associates and S. Goldberg and Associates. His firm is the recipient of numerous awards, including the Chicago Sun-Times Award for Best City Development and The Home Builders Association of Greater Chicago Award for Outstanding Residential Design.

FitzGerald Associates Architects worked on Centennial Court and Park Row at Central Station. Patrick FitzGerald leads the third generation of the firm that began in 1919 as Rissman & Hirschfield and later became

Reinheimer & Associates. Today FitzGerald Associates Arvhitects is known for buildings that combine striking variations of traditional designs with an innovative and efficient use of space.

PFDA, a division of The Daly Group, is an innovative architectural and land planning organization that is working on the proposed Promenade on Michigan Avenue and the building on the 1300 block. The firm was formed in 1975 and has since been involved in more than $1 billion of construction in 29 states. Additionally, PFDA has been honored with awards from the Association of Licensed Architects.

Pappageorge/Haymes Ltd., were the archtects of Museum Park, Museum Park Lofts, and Grant Park Tower. The firm previously played a major role in the development of 600 North Lake Shore Drive, 840 North Lake Shore Drive, University Village, Old Town Square, Orchard Park, West Market Place, and the Kenwood/Oakland Master Plan among its most significant projects.

Dick Mann of Mann, Gin, Dubin & Frazier, Ltd., a Chicago-based architectural firm established in 1977, designed Senior Suites/Central Station for Senior Lifestyle Corporation. The firm has been responsible for the space planning, design and construction administration for numerous senior citizens residential developments, includ-

ing The Breakers at Edgewater Beach and Olympia Fields, Mangrove Bay in Jupiter, Florida; Senior Suites throughout Chicago, including Central Station, and residential high-rises including the 48-story New Yorker in Chicago. The firm has also completed a significant number of projects for the Chicago Board of Education, the Chicago Park District, the City of Chicago, City Colleges of Chicago and the Metropolitan Pier and Exposition Authority.

Ehrenkrantz Eckstut & Kuhn was the original master planner for Central Station. The firm, founded in 1959, has an unusually diverse national practice with offices in New York, Los Angeles and Washington D.C. and an extensive portfolio of award-winning designs for every type of urban building. EE&K is a highly diversified and innovative architectural firm that emphasizes complex, mixed-use developments. Among its most notworthy projects are Metrotech, Circle Centre, Battery Park City, Gateway Center, and The Dakota. The diversity of styles evident in the firm's work represents its ability to convey a range of responses.

Solomon Cordwell Buenz & Associates served as the planner for Central Station's proposed venture with Russia. The firm was established in 1931and evolved into a practice whose main concentration and expertise is in office, educational, multifamily residential, hotel, retail, institutional and transportation facilities. In addition to new construction projects, SCB has considerable expertise in adaptive rehabilitation of existing structures. Based in Chicago, the firm has worked throughout the United States. Among its more recognized projects are The Bristol in Chicago; CityFront Terrace in San Diego; One Embarcadero Place in San Francisco; Northwestern University Kemper Hall, Evanston; Sun Wall Competition, Department of Energy, Washington, DC; and Oakbrook Center Phase III Expansion in Oak Brook, Illinois.

Warman Olsen Warman Ltd was the architect for Prairie District Homes. Formed in 1983 as a full service architectural design firm, Warman Olsen Warman has successfuly completed projects for healthcare, residential, retail, hospitality, commercial, industrial, correctional, academic and municipal facilities. The firm's clients have included Abbott Laboratories, the Army Corps of Engineers, Stein & Company, Grand Metropolitan Hotels, Hyatt Development Corporation, the Palmer House Hilton, Loyola University Medical Center, Bally's Inc., Historic Homes Ltd., and Legacy Development Group.

Daniel Weinbach & Partners, landscape architects, is a full service landscape architectural firm in Chicago. The firm's portfolio includes local, national and international projects that range in type and scale from large corporate campuses to small private gardens. Among its shocase projects is Daniel Webster Park at Central Station.

About the Authors

Gerald W. Fogelson is the Founder and President of The Fogelson Companies and the co-chairman and CEO of Central Station Development Corporation. He is a major builder and developer in Chicago and is nationally known as an innovative and talented expert in mixed use projects of all types, having developed thousands of rental apartments, shopping centers, industrial parks, office buildings, marina properties and themed communities, including a large equestrian project, as well as houses and condominiums.

Fogelson began his career during his senior year at Lehigh University in Bethlehem, Pa., building houses that sold for $9,900—including the cost of the lot.

He is a member of the Board of Trustees of Mt. Sinai Hospital; a trustee of Roosevelt University; a member of the Near South Planning Board; co-chairman of the Board of Advisors and founder of the Chicago School of Real Estate at Roosevelt University; and is active in numerous civic and philanthropic efforts.

In 1988, Jerry Fogelson put the Illinois Central's 69-acre property under contract to develop what is now one of America's largest urban developments. *Central Station: Realizing a Vision* is his story. This is his first book.

Joe Marconi is a writer and the author of eleven books, including *Crisis Marketing: When Bad Things Happen to Good Companies* and the novel, *Getting There*. He is based in Western Springs, Illinois, near Chicago.

Bibliography

Chicago: A Century of Progress A commemorative volume, author and copyright date unknown.Chicago: Marquette Publishing Company.

Chicago: Growth of a Metropolis by Harold M. Mayer and Richard C. Wade. Chicago and London: University of Chicago Press, 1969.

Chicago Sun-Times: ""World's Tallest Building" by David Roeder, July 18, 2001.

Chicago Tribune: "Central Station gathers steam" by J. Linn Allen, October 14, 1999; "On-fire Station— Mega development lights a new spark under residential building in the hot South Loop" by John Handley, May 7, 2000; "These towers offer trendline for South Loop" by Genevieve Buck, August 4, 2001.

City of the Century: The Epic of Chicago and the Making of America by Donald L. Miller.New York: Simon & Schuster, 1996.

Constructing Chicago by Daniel Bluestone. New Haven and London: Yale University Press, 1991.

Crain's Chicago Business: "Giant Step for South Loop" by Thomas A. Corfman, March 8, 1998; "New housing push set for S. Loop site" by Thomas A. Corfman, December 6, 1999;

Forever Open, Clear and Free by Lois Wille. Chicago: Henry RegneryCompany, 1972.

Limiteds Along the Lakefront: The Illinois Central in Chicago by Alan R. Lind. Park Forest, IL: Transport History Press, 1986.

They Built Chicago: Entrepreneurs Who Shaped A Great City's Architecture by Miles Berger. Chicago: Bonus Books, 1992.

Index